The Special Needs SCHOOL Survival Guide

Handbook for Autism, Sensory Processing Disorder, ADHD, Learning Disabilities & More!

Cara Koscinski MOT, OTR/L
The Pocket Occupational Therapist

The Special Needs SCHOOL Survival Guide:
Handbook for Autism, Sensory Processing Disorder, ADHD, Learning Disabilities & More!

All marketing and publishing rights guaranteed to and reserved by:

FUTURE HORIZONSINC.

721 W Abram St, Arlington, TX 76013
800-489-0727 (toll free)
817-277-0727 (local)
817-277-2270 (fax)
E-mail: info@fhautism.com
www.fhautism.com

ISBN: 9781941765210

Dedication

To J and J:
Being your mom has taught and blessed me
more than I could have ever imagined.

Most importantly, I now understand that anything is possible
if you work hard enough and find joy in the situation.

"There will be haters, there will be doubters,
there will be non-believers
and then there will be YOU, proving them wrong."
-Unknown

Contents

Acknowledgments

A very special thank you to all of those students I've been blessed to work with. You have taught me to be creative and think outside of the box. I've learned something from EVERY one of you! Most importantly, I think of you all as children who needed a little help to unwrap your gifts.

This book would not have been possible without the support of my family. B, thank you for honoring my requests of quiet time, and indulging my constant passion for OT and writing. J and J, homeschooling has meant more to me than you'll ever know. The time spent teaching you has been a true blessing!

Angie, I thank your for your advice with publishing and your kindness. I admire you and all of your contributions to our field.

To Marie, your constant support and enthusiasm for the field of OT has been contagious! You're ALWAYS willing to endorse my work. I am blessed to know you.

Dad and Mom, you believed in me from the day I decided to become an OT. Even though I received a FULL scholarship to a university which did not have OT as a major; you provided me with a private and expensive education to fulfill my OT dreams. I'm forever grateful.

To my autism e-mail buddies, I love connecting and laughing with you! What a great group of ladies.

Last, but never least, is my sister. Kim, words escape me, and all I can say is that you're my world! I love you.

Introduction

As I raise my own children with special needs, I am always in search of publications that will give me a feeling of empowerment. It's with that thought in mind that I write my own books. As The Pocket Occupational Therapist, it's my desire to provide you with the most up-to-date and comprehensive information. Every book is meant to assist you not only to use techniques, but to understand the why behind them. Teaching the caregiver is my passion.

Parenting, teaching, and/or working with students who have special needs is a true gift. Please remember that every child develops at his own pace and one student should never be compared with another. Always consider the student's developmental level; not his age level. Many students, even those without special needs, acquire skills at their own pace. We are all unique! Additionally, remember to work as a team for the benefit of the child.

Not everyone who teaches a child with special needs also lives with one (or more) of these awesome kids. It's by living with and working with students who have special needs that I've learned so very much. Resources are listed at the end of most chapters. I've been objective and have provided a comprehensive list of websites and references. No monetary compensation has been given to me by any of the resources in exchange for listing them in my book. I have, however, had the privilege of using some of the products for my own students throughout the years.

Please note that every disability comes with unique challenges and I cannot possibly list every one. The same is true for accommodations. No list is exhaustive and we all learn more and more from each other every day. Feel free to add your own ideas in the "Notes" section.

This book is not a substitute for medical advice. I urge you to consult your individual health professional or occupational therapist prior to beginning any of the activities or programs listed in this book.

I sincerely thank you for reading!

Many blessings,
Cara

Chapter 1

IEP 101—What You Need to Know

About IEPs and 504 Plans; What Are IEPs?

The acronym IEP stands for Individualized Education Program. It was derived from the Individuals with Disabilities Education Act (IDEA). Once qualified under this act, the child (according to part b of the IDEA) qualifies for a Free and Appropriate Public Education (FAPE). Each student between the ages of three and twenty-two should have access to general and special education services free of charge. Additionally, the student with disabilities must have access to the same educational services as students without disabilities. This rule includes extra-curricular events. A student with special needs may also qualify for a behavioral intervention plan. The plan is administered along with the regulations of the IDEA law. Remember though, all students are responsible for following the rules of their school districts, but if the student with an IEP requires disciplinary action, the team must discuss whether or not the student's disability contributed to his behavior. It is quite complex and is far from black and white, so it's important to understand your student's rights.

To qualify for this program through the IDEA law, the student must have one or more of the disabilities listed. There are thirteen of them. (Please refer to www.wrightslaw.com for details.) The key is that the disability must adversely affect the student's performance in school/education. As a result of the disability, the child needs specialized education services to make progress in school and to benefit from the general education program. The purpose of any IEP must be to provide a program that is specifically tailored to each student's needs. The IEP refers both to the meeting held to make the document and the actual document created at that meeting. The goals specified within it must be measureable with smaller and more detailed goals (called short-term goals). The IEP needs to be updated every three years, if not before. The IDEA also outlines what options a family has if they disagree with the outcomes of the IEP meeting. According to the Rehabilitation Act of 1973, there may be no discrimination of any student going to a school which is federally funded. The key is that the disability substantially limits major life activities. Another law, the Americans with Disabilities Act (ADA) applies to education because its goal is to prevent discrimination against those with disabilities. Additionally, Congress updated the IDEA in 2009 to ensure that all accommodations which were previously not documented must now be formalized. It's important to note that plans are included if students attend a school that is government funded.

What Should I Do if I Think My Student Needs an IEP?

It's your right to investigate and learn how your student is performing in school. You can communicate with teachers, ask for progress reports/tests/work samples, and even visit the school to observe your student in the classroom. Most parents are unaware that there may be additional programs available to children who need them. It is important to be polite and respectful to school staff. However, know your rights as a tax-paying citizen.

When parents suspect that their child needs additional support to learn, the parent's next step is to request an evaluation for an IEP in writing. Sometimes, the school staff/teachers will recommend an evaluation. You will be notified of their request and will be asked to sign a paper asking for permission/consent for evaluation.

Out of the Pocket Activity

I have had the benefit of sitting through hundreds of IEP meetings over the years. It's been quite interesting to attend as the parent, advocate, and OT! Thankfully, there are quite a few helpful ideas I've learned.

If you are mailing the request for an IEP evaluation, send it via certified mail. This way, you will be certain that the school has signed for and received your request. Any formal documentation you keep as a parent will prove helpful if any difficulties arise. As with any other situation, creating a paper trail will be quite beneficial. My theory is that if it's not written down, it didn't happen! I highly recommend purchasing a three ring binder solely for IEP-related documents. The binder should contain school information and district policy on IEP; your child's strengths and weaknesses; a copy of the Procedural Safeguards Notice (see next section); professional evaluations and reports relating to your child's diagnosis; current level of function; any classroom observations you've done; and any medical needs. Despite many nightmare stories you may have heard about IEPs, with a positive attitude and by developing a good relationship with the school district, a wonderful plan is possible.

What Do I Need to Know Before the Evaluation and IEP?

After it is determined that your student will be evaluated, the school is required by law to give parents a copy of the "Procedural Safeguards Notice." This document informs caregivers and parents what legal rights they have in order to make sure that their student receives the services that he or she needs. In the US, the CPIR (Center for Parent Information and Resources) www.parentcenterhub. org is a wonderful site as it provides information about where you can find help in your state if you have any questions. Since each state has different rules and timelines, it's critical to familiarize yourself with the specific timelines in your state for evaluation, IEP meetings, annual updates, etc. The Procedural Safeguards Notice is to be in the native language of the parents. I recommend this is kept in the IEP binder for future reference as well. If you lose or misplace it, you have the right to ask for the document at any time. School districts often post this information on their websites for easier reference. The more you know as the caregiver, the better you will be able to advocate for your student. Isn't this the best policy every time?

According to the National Center, "Schools must provide a copy of the Procedural Safeguards Notice[1]:

- Upon initial referral or parental request for evaluation;
- Once each school year (for students eligible for IDEA services);
- When parents first file a complaint (either a state complaint or due process complaint);
- When the student is removed from his or her current educational placement because of a violation of a code of conduct;
- Upon request by the parent."

What Is Included in the IEP Evaluation?

Before we discuss the actual evaluation, it is important to let you know that the school must discuss what the evaluation will entail. If you feel that there are specific areas of testing or types of assessments your student may need, you have the right to mention your concerns to the evaluation team. Additionally, you may object to any test you do not want completed. The evaluation must use proven testing in many areas; it should include teacher input; should include any previous data collected on your student; and should consider all areas of disability. Most people don't know that the evaluation must be completed in the student's native language to ensure he understands all of the tasks asked of him.

The school district has 45 days (from the date of request to evaluate, according to www.wrightslaw.com.) to evaluate the student and produce a report for the review of the team and parent. Once the evaluation process is completed, the report must be provided within a specific time frame. According to Nolo's IEP Guide: Learning Disabilities (Siegel, L. 2003) (2), the "initial IEP meeting must be held within 30 days after the school district determines your child is eligible for special education." The team must inform and invite the parent/caregiver to the meeting with a letter and the date/time/location of the team meeting must be convenient for both the school and the parent(s). Parents are encouraged to participate in the evaluation and referral process as well as attend IEP, annual, and review meetings.

Each state/district may have specific time line requirements. Remember that states must follow Federal law, but can have additional stipulations. Reference the website above (CPIR - Center for Parent Information and Resources at www.parentcenterhub.org) for your state's requirements.

If you'd prefer to do so, you may choose to have an independent assessment done by someone suggested by your pediatrician. However, the school district does not have to pay for that evaluation. When your child is having the first or initial evaluation to determine IEP eligibility, you may have the school complete it or you may choose to pay for an independent evaluation on your own. Additionally, you may or may not choose to provide a copy of the independent evaluation to the school. Remember, the more information the team has about your student, the better the plan will be.

Every parent has the right to view and have a copy of the evaluation done by the school. Request a copy in writing. If you do not deliver the request personally, send your letter certified for proof of delivery. The results of the evaluation may be disputed or challenged by the family. I recommend you thoroughly read and review the report. Highlight things you agree with in one color and results you do not agree with or do not understand in another color. Write all questions down in the margin for easy reference later.

> NOTE: If a parent does not agree with the initial (first) evaluation provided by the school district, they have the right to request a second outside evaluation. This second evaluation must be approved by the team and must be completed using the same standards that the school district has. Discuss this with the district prior to having the evaluation done as they must agree to the conditions of this second evaluation if you want them to pay for it.

What Can I Expect at the IEP Meeting?

The IEP meeting can often bring about feelings of stress. Of course, you want to create the best possible plan for your student. Find out ahead of time who will be attending the meeting. Ensure you take along the binder I discussed earlier in this chapter. It's fine to bring a support person who will help you to feel confident and relaxed. It is your legal right to have an advocate present who is familiar with the IEP process. Often, having someone with you gives you another set of eyes and ears in the meeting.

The caregiver or legal guardian, regular education teacher, special education teacher, school/local education administrator, the student, and other professionals who are determined to be necessary by the team will attend the IEP. Some may serve double roles, for example, the school principal may be the education administrator. Other individuals may be the OT, SLP (Speech Language Pathologist), PT (Physical Therapist), a translator, aides, autism specialist, social worker, psychologist, anyone you would like to attend, reading specialists, low-vision specialists, and many more depending on your student.

Additionally, make sure you are familiar with the language used in the IEP and if possible, do some research on sites such as the NCLD (National Center for Learning Disabilities (www.NCLD.org); Wrightslaw (www.wrightslaw.com); and School Psychology (school-psychology.org). The 1997 update to IDEA (Individuals with Disabilities Education Act) outlines the required content for what needs to be contained within an IEP. The following site has downloadable PDF or Word documents on the US Department of Education's website (www.ed.gov) which outlines the requirements.

IEPs have several required components. The following information should be included in the IEP:

- identifying information;
- present levels of academic achievement and functional performance
  It's very important to ensure this is correct as it is the level at which the student is currently functioning. Review and discuss any disagreements with the IEP team;
- what makes the student eligible or how he is affected in school by the disability;
- behavior interventions/plans;
- English proficiency, communication, visual or hearing impairments;
- measurable annual goals and objectives with short-term benchmarks;
- special education, related services, and supplementary aids and services;
- amount of time students will participate in general education classes and

the best way to meet the student's needs in general education (including extra-curricular activities);

- participation in state or district-wide academic assessments (including accommodations to be provided and reasons for using an alternate assessment if the child will not participate in the regular assessment);
- initiation date and projected duration of IEP;
- transition services (students aged fourteen and older);
- how student progress toward annual goals will be measured and how/when periodic reports will be provided to parents;
- when students will have access to and participation in the general curriculum;
- whether or not the student qualifies for ESY (extended school year).

All states must follow Federal requirements and states may have additional regulations. In fact, each state is required to have a special education advisory commission. Please contact your state's CPIR (Center for Parent Information and Resources www.parentcenterhub.org) for the state's commission and for updates to special education law.

It is important to know that you do not have to sign the IEP if you disagree with it. You need to sign only the attendance form that you were present at the IEP. Some parents sign the IEP and note next to their signature that they do not agree with the plan. If you choose not to sign agreement of the IEP document, take it home, review it, and make notes about what you do and do not agree with. Write your disagreements down and add your signature. Please check www.Wrightslaw. com website for help with what to do when you disagree with the IEP as the IDEA requires "due process" hearings when disagreements occur. This is a complicated topic and since I'm not an attorney, here's a reference to an excellent resource for IEP information and legal information is *Nolo's IEP Guide: Learning Disabilities* (5th edition) by Attorney Lawrence M. Siegel. It's available wherever books are sold. (3)

What Is a 504 Plan?

One of the most frequently asked questions I receive is about the difference between IEPs and 504 plans. A 504 plan originated from a civil-rights law, the Rehabilitation Act of 1973 (section 504). The benefit is to remove any barrier that would prohibit students with disabilities to participate freely in education. Students who qualify for IEPs (remember, they are under the Individuals with Disabilities Education Act, or IDEA) require far more assistance to participate in their education. In essence, students who do not qualify for the classifications in the IDEA, but require some additional help to be able to fully participate in school may receive a 504 plan. The 504 plan and the Americans with Disabilities Act (ADA) help to protect all students from discrimination due to their disabilities.

What is considered a disability under section 504? Any student who has a physical or mental impairment that may limit one or more major life activities are regarded as having an impairment; or has any record/documentation of an impairment qualifies. Any disability that's documented, such as food allergies, feeding tubes, diabetes, wheelchair/walker/crutches use, among many others will qualify. Remember, you have the right to request an evaluation by the school district to determine if your student will qualify for either an IEP or 504 plan.

The 504 is a list of specific accommodations that must be made for the student who needs them. There must be removal of all barriers in the regular education program for these students. Also, there is no funding from the IDEA for these supports. Either the school or the parents can request an evaluation. If the school requests it, the parents should be notified that the evaluation is taking place. Additionally, the evaluation must have input from a variety of sources, including those involved in the student's education. When the meeting occurs for the 504 plan, the team comes together to discuss the accommodations which would best benefit the student. In essence, most of the accommodations listed in this book (with the exception of specific educational placements) may apply and be included in the student's 504 plan.

In my experience, there are some school districts that prepare a standard list of accommodations for a specific diagnosis and there is no such list. The purpose of the 504 plan is to look at the specific needs of the child being considered. Since every child is different, every 504 plan should be. Make sure you communicate with the team to see how the plan is working and re-evaluate the accommodations and plan annually (if not before).

Did you know that section 504 applies to colleges and adults in the workplace? It's true! Anyone working for or attending a school which accepts federal funding must make accommodations for anyone who qualifies for the civil-rights law, the Rehabilitation Act of 1973 (section 504). Many people do not know their rights according to the law. It is for this reason that you should continue to meet with the guidance/counseling team in college and provide them with a copy of the most current 504 plan. Make sure to keep it updated in college because your employer needs to make these same accommodations for you too! This is very exciting and many people do not realize the benefits of this law throughout their lifetime! There are many ways to have the best and most successful life possible. Know your rights and never stop asking questions or advocating for yourself.

What Is the Difference between an Accommodation and a Modification?

An accommodation is a change in the way a teacher delivers the target skill information (the concepts which are being taught) to the student; the response given by the student; the way in which the student responds and answers to demonstrate they understand; the time given for tests and assignments; the setting in which the student takes tests. We do not change the goals for the student's education. For example, Jennifer has difficulty with distractions in the classroom when she is taking a test. Her IEP allows for the accommodations of taking the test in a quiet setting (guidance office) with additional time. Another student with sensory processing disorder has difficulty sitting still during science class. Her IEP allows for the accommodation of going to the sensory room or completing physical activities for 20 minutes prior to science. It also permits the use of a Tangle® fidget toy during class time. If Richard has low-vision, we can increase the print on worksheets, use a magnifier, or read material to him. There are many different accommodations for students and of course, they must be individualized by student, agreed on by the team, and listed in the IEP or 504 plan.

A modification is an actual change in the target skill (concept or material being taught). If we are modifying the instruction material, we are changing what we teach to the student. This is often the case when our students cannot work on grade level. Tyler is in seventh grade in most subjects, but in language arts, he functions at a fourth grade level. His IEP provides a modification that he will work from fourth grade textbooks and with special education instruction at his functional level. Modifications decrease the expectations we have for a student. They change the actual academic goals we expect. When modifications are made, we reduce the expectations about a student's performance. Self-contained classrooms often have modified curriculums.

Can You Provide Me with a List of Some Common Accommodations?

The IEP or 504 plan accommodations must be specific to your child's needs and agreed upon by the team members attending the meeting. In each chapter, I have listed accommodations for specific needs or disabilities. There are generally five categories we can use to group accommodations: Scheduling, setting, instruction, student response, and timing. Here are several examples of accommodations:

- Break down projects into more manageable steps.
- Allow students to have extra time for testing or to turn in homework.
- Preferred seating near the teacher or board.
- Allow tests to be taken in a different area such as a quiet office.
- Permit students to use a standing table for classwork.
- Use multi-sensory techniques for teaching new concepts.
- Add a tutor.
- Add seating, e.g., small air discs, ball chairs, or T Stools.
- Permit manipulatives to teach math concepts.
- Use of a keyboard/computer vs. handwriting
- Write on special paper with adaptations of lines, color, and spacing.
- Use visual organizers, charts, schedules.
- Provide sensory adaptations for fidgeting with hands and body.
- Change the writing utensil.
- Provide an additional set of books for home.
- Add a communication book about homework for the team, including parents.
- Use teacher's lecture notes to study.
- Limit the number of problems that the student answers for homework. For example: complete only odd or even problems.
- Do not grade for neatness on homework and tests.
- Allow earplugs or noise-cancelling headphones.
- Add a reward system.
- Enlarge materials for low-vision.
- Use word processors.
- Additional warning of transitions, fire or disaster drills.
- Provide a sensory space or sensory diet.
- Allow for use of standing tables, beanbag chairs, or other seating.
- Change the color of the paper used for worksheets.

- Offer stress management training for students.
- Provide help with goal setting and time management.

Keep reading for your student's specific area of weakness. You'll find many helpful accommodations.

What Are Some Types of Classroom Placements for My Student?

The ultimate goal of the educational plan is to ensure that a student is placed into the least restrictive environment for learning. The No Child Left Behind law specifies that a child must be in the most inclusive setting. This simply means that we do not want to isolate students simply because they have a learning disability or special need. Each student has the right to be educated in a safe, non-threatening, enriching classroom.

The first type of classroom is called mainstream. Students who are mainstreamed are placed within the regular education classroom with peers at the same age/grade. There may or may not be a special education teacher present, but according to the IEP, goals are in place and data is taken. Accommodations will be in place to ensure the student has the tools for success within the classroom.

A resource room is used when the student is generally in the mainstream classroom and needs additional help with a certain subject(s). The special education teacher is trained to provide helpful strategies for students with specific special needs or learning disabilities. Resource rooms have small groups of students and provide the additional help that a student needs for success. For some of the day or for some difficult subjects, the student moves to the resource room. The student's IEP will dictate which subjects and what length of time your student will have this additional help.

Self-contained classrooms are structured rooms where a student goes for the entire school day. The classroom has a special education teacher and the student may work on a unique curriculum or out of different books than he would if in the general education classroom. There are many benefits to a self-contained classroom such as: students receive individualized help, the curriculum they are working on is adapted specifically for the student, and students may be in the safest environment for them.

Most Restrictive—Education in a special education classroom that is self-contained. Likely using modified curriculum.

Few inclusive services in general education. Activities with special education support, and academic instruction occurs primarily in the special education setting.

Inclusive services in some general education subjects and activities with support from special education teacher. Collaborative model allows general ed. and special ed. teachers to work together. Small group instruction within classroom.

Inclusive services in all general education subjects and activities with no support from the special education teacher.

There is also an option of placing students in a school specialized for their individual needs. Some schools specialize in autism, in ADHD/ADD, or dyslexia (learning disabilities). There are even schools which specialize in gifted education! If there is a school available for your student, make sure to research it and discuss transportation. Every district has rules for placement, so the best thing is to educate yourself on the best option for your student.

What Can Go Wrong at the IEP/504?

Is there anything I can do to help avoid a mistake in the meeting?

There are many things that can go wrong in any meeting. When two or more people get together to discuss anything, there can be disagreements. The unique thing about IEP and 504 plan meetings is that we are all thinking about the best outcomes for a unique student/person. The goal of everyone should be the student's welfare. Of course, this is the real world and there are many things that can hinder a meeting. Consideration for a school budget, misperception of the difference between school and clinic- based therapy, thinking of the impact on the other students in the classroom, not knowing the law/rights, a parent's anger over a new "diagnosis" or "label" for the student, etc. can all cause disagreements or raise concerns.

OUT OF THE POCKET ACTIVITY

- Enter the meeting with a positive attitude. Do not assume that the school is "out to get you" because you've been an advocate for your child.
- Read all of the evaluations from the therapists, psychologists, school, etc. prior to the meeting. Highlight the areas that you do not agree with and request corrections. Requests should be written down.
- Bring someone with you. I always bring a supportive family member, advocate, or friend with me for support. It's also good to ask that person to take notes and for reviewing the events which occurred at the meeting with someone afterward. I suggest going for coffee or lunch to discuss and process the meeting's events, the plan, etc. You can choose to have an attorney present if you wish.
- Do not scream or yell at school staff. When you disagree, try to keep calm

and speak clearly. Take deep breaths when upset or ask for a brief break.

- Never sign anything of which you're not 100% clear. Ask questions and make sure you understand exactly what's being suggested for your student. It's your right to ask for clarification and to understand why your student is being placed into a certain setting, receiving therapy, or what the goals mean. Do not sign the plan at the meeting if you do not agree with it. Request to read it afterwards and make certain you review it to ensure you've understood it clearly.

- Every area of weakness should have a goal addressing it. It's equally important to know who or which service is working on each goal. There is no limit on the number of goals for any student.

- The goals and IEP should be written specifically for your student. The goals should be specific to each student's areas of weakness. There is no such thing as a cookie-cutter or standard IEP or 504 plan. Additionally, the placement of the student should be agreed upon during the meeting.

- Ensure that everything discussed at the meeting including any changes suggested and any changes you request need to be made in writing. I tell everyone I work with, "If it's not written down, it did not happen and can be denied."

Chapter 1 Resources

www.autismspeaks	Autism Speaks
www.ed.gov	US Dept. of Education
www.nea.org	National Education Association
www.NCLD.org	National Center for Learning Disabilities
www.parentcenterhub.org	Center for Parent Information & Resources
www.wrightslaw.com	Wrightslaw

Chapter 2

Therapy in School

What Is Therapy in the School Setting?

Not all children who attend outpatient or clinic therapy will qualify for therapy in the school setting. It is critical to realize that in order to receive therapy in school, the child's area of weakness must directly impact function in the educational setting. Furthermore, when a therapist is in a school setting, he/she must write goals which are "educationally relevant." Therapists in the schools have different roles than those in outpatient clinics. It's our job to assist students to function in their regular and special education classroom.

There are times in a school setting when the therapist is "consulting" or providing helpful suggestions based on observations and data. The purpose of the consultative model is to identify and collaborate with school staff/resources to provide suggestions and ways to modify the environment/situation for optimal success. The suggestions are meant for improved functional skills in the classroom, during transition times, with center times (for younger students), for planning/organizing, with grip on pencil or scissors, or for visual-perceptual work. The therapist is working with the people who teach the student, the aide or other staff, but not directly with the student when doing consultation. Additionally, when a therapist is working on goals for carry-over, he must ensure the staff working with the student is well-trained.

Another model for providing therapy is by direct service. When a therapist is performing direct services, he/she is working with the student to learn new skills and this usually takes place in the therapy room or quiet area of the classroom. The therapist is using hands-on techniques and focuses solely on the student's needs and goals. For example, when working on pencil grip, the therapist may be using putty with small objects placed inside to increase hand strength. Next, they practice using the appropriate pre-writing strokes of forming lines. This is not taking place with the other students in the classroom since the student needs to focus and receive the therapist's individual attention. However, a therapist may have other students in a small group with their targeted student. This is often the case when a speech-language pathologist is working on social skills training.

Some districts use integrated service models. This means that therapists are working hands-on with the student among her peers in her natural environment. The individual student is receiving services to improve functional/academic skills and achieve goals in the targeted area of weakness. Here's an example: the OT may be working on cutting with the student while she's at center time with her peers.

It is important to note whether a therapist is performing consultative or direct services, because she must always take data on the student's progress to provide necessary information for IEP goal monitoring. Additionally, law mandates that IEPs be reviewed annually and/or at least every three years. The student must receive services in the least restrictive environment. It can be confusing for caregivers to know what may qualify for school therapy services, so please consult your individual therapist or your district or state regulations. They can usually be found on the district's website, but it's your right to know these regulations, so ask for a copy.

What Are Some Signs My Student May Need Therapy?

There are many strategies wonderful teachers use with all students or those who may show signs of struggle that are not part of an individualized education plan. They are called "pre-referral interventions." Schools have been using different approaches to use research-based instruction. Response to Intervention (RTI) is a multi-tiered approach divided into three support levels and the intensity increases with each level. Visit the site: www.rtinetwork.org for information. The site is extremely helpful and explains RTI in clear terms.

Other pre-referral interventions may be done. They may include something such as posting a visual schedule of the school day on the board or copying tests onto only one side of the paper. Often times, after a parent/teacher meeting, the team may agree that some minor changes in school or at homework time will work well. When common strategies have been tried and failed, it may be time for some extra help from a therapist. Please document the things that worked well for your student; did not work well; behaviors the student had when you tried the strategy; or questions you have.

Look for the following signs in different areas where a student may benefit from skilled therapy intervention.

OUT OF THE POCKET ACTIVITY

- has more difficulty than other children with self-care activities such as: tying shoes, getting jackets on/off, toileting, set-up or clean-up of lunch;
- avoids or refuses to complete center craft activities;

- exhibits behaviors that are not age appropriate when doing independent work (tantrums, making loud noises with mouth, getting up frequently to sharpen pencil during the time allotted);
- does not initiate speech or social interactions with other students;
- cannot re-tell a story or provide details after reading a passage;
- has difficulty navigating stairs, gym class, and hallways;
- cannot transfer from place to place without falling;
- avoids learning new skills and skills in the classroom;
- has difficulty walking in line or being close to children;
- does not participate in recess and gym activities;
- has difficulty organizing desk and homework materials;
- demonstrates increased difficulty copying work from the board;
- forgets assignments or seems disorganized;
- difficulty with handwriting, using a pen/pencil, forming letters and numbers, forming cursive letters;
- has trouble with the use of tools such as scissors, hole punchers, staplers;
- demonstrates frequent tantrums when tasks are difficult;
- places objects in mouth frequently such as clothing, classroom items, toys;
- has difficulty with following commands or classroom routines;
- does not know left from right;
- avoids getting messy with items such as glue and paint;
- difficulty sitting still and seems in "constant motion";
- has trouble making friends;
- seems to get lost easily in the school building or when transitioning between activities;
- difficulty playing independently at recess or reckless/impulsive behavior;
- difficulty maintaining upright posture in her chair or during circle time;
- has visual-spatial trouble.

The list above is not exhaustive, but is meant to show examples of what difficulties a student may have. Remember that there are many variations in the time each child acquires skills. For example, if a child has a condition affecting his development, there may be a discrepancy between his actual age and his functional age levels. For example, it is important to note if a particular child is performing academic work well beyond his age expectations, but needs extra help to make friends or remember classroom routines.

Difficulty with activities of daily living (ADLs) are often an indicator of the need for additional therapy. Things such as re-dressing after toileting, blowing nose, opening/closing containers, using toilet, washing hands, opening/closing doors, putting on/taking off jacket, managing backpack, walking, navigating stairs or gym class, setting up lunch and feeding self independently are all activities that a child is required to do independently in school. Remember, these skills may be emerging for pre-k and kindergarten students. Teachers are wonderfully insightful as to whether or not skills are developing appropriately in the classroom.

What Is Occupational Therapy?

Occupational therapists (OTs) are critical members of the team in both medical and school settings. OTs work to ensure the student can perform activities of daily living as independently as possible. There are several areas in school where OTs can make a significant impact. Through a thorough evaluation in areas such as: fine motor, strength, vision and perceptual skills, sensory processing, and more; goals will be developed specifically for your student. Areas that are also considered include: overall transition skills, direction following, organization, attention, and self-care as it relates to education. The time an OT works with a student directly depends on the time that the team determines is necessary to participate in his education with the appropriate accommodations and supports. When parents, teachers, therapists, and students are aware of the tools available to them, it is beneficial to everyone in building the best educational plan. OTs are part of the "related services" category – part b in the Individuals with Disabilities Education Act.

What Are Some Common OT Goals in the School Setting?

In addition to the list of activities in the previous section, many districts are recognizing the importance of SPD (sensory processing disorder) and its impact on a child's daily routine. Here is an example of an OT goal which would cover SPD relating to a child's educational needs: By the end of the IEP date, Jacob will demonstrate the ability to regulate his body for quiet work tasks by choosing an appropriate calming down activity 90% of the time. The therapist may teach Jacob how to monitor his level of "alertness" with a program such as *How Does Your Engine Run?*® by Shelly Shellenberger and Mary Sue Williams (www.alertprogram.com)[4]. Further, he may then learn which activities in the program are calming to him vs. causing him to become more active when he and his peers are doing quiet work at their desks. I have created a series of activity cards or sensory break cards on my website which are inexpensive and easy to download, print, and laminate. They are colorful and a great visual reminder for students with and without special needs! (www.pocketot.com, under the "shop" tab)

Here are some sample annual goals in an IEP:

- In a one year period, Mary will stabilize the paper with one hand while drawing and writing to compose language arts lessons 75% of the time.
- By the end of the IEP, Victor will be able to isolate a finger to push a button, keyboard, mouse, etc. to type 26 out of 26 lowercase letters 100% of the time in ELA class.
- At the end of the IEP period, Jennifer will demonstrate the ability to hold

her writing utensil with a tripod grasp during writing class 75% of the time as evidenced by data collection by OT.

- In one year, Joshua will demonstrate the ability to use proper spacing between words during ELA class when writing 90% of the time.
- Billy will be able to copy math assignments at his desk to record 100% of the assignment during this IEP period.
- Jeremy will complete math tasks regardless of external visual stimulation 70% of the time, by 1/2/16.
- When frustrated during science lessons, Virginia will use relaxation techniques to regulate arousal level 90% of the time, according to data collected by Ms. Jones.

Every goal needs to note who is collecting the data and monitoring the progress. The goals we write need to be measureable and they need to be given a time frame (the annual IEP period for long-term goals). The goals need to be broken down into smaller, more measureable goals. They are called "short-term goals (STG)." They are like steps which show progress toward the long term goal. Here's an example:

The long-term goal will be: In one year from the date of this IEP, Richard will cut curved lines, including circles accurately within ⅛ inch of the line independently.

- STG 1: Richard will use scissors to cut along the curved line within 1 inch from the line 100% of the time.
- STG 2: Richard will use scissors to cut along the curved line within ½ inch from the line 100% of the time.
- STG 3: Richard will use scissors to cut along the curved line within ¼ inch from the line 100% of the time.

Data is collected on goals in most districts on a quarterly basis, just as progress reports are. The timing is near the school's quarterly report cards. Therapists, teachers, and those collecting data make notes in the student's record how she is progressing toward every IEP goal at that time. You may view this data and ask questions about your student.

What Is Language?
What Is a Speech-Language Pathologist?

Language is much more than having the ability to speak. If we think of sign language, there is a beautiful flowing rhythm with facial expressions and body movements. Our verbal language is the same. We use gestures, facial expressions, vocal tones, eye contact, body movements (such as pointing and hand position) to communicate ideas and thoughts. When a child struggles with social communication deficits, language/speech delays, autism, strokes, neurological injuries, and many more; their social skills may suffer. To communicate with each other, we must understand taking turns, the appropriate way to get someone's attention, body language, conversational turn-taking, facial expressions, sarcasm, idioms, eye contact, and intonation. All of these make up the pragmatics of speech.

There can be delays in either receptive language (understanding), expressive language, or both. To complicate things even more, our language is full of idioms (it's raining cats and dogs), homophones (hear and here), and sarcasm. Those who are developing typically can become frustrated!

Speech-language pathologists (SLPs) are experts in the area of speech and communication and are vital members of the treatment team. They are part of the "related services" category – part b under the Individuals with Disabilities Education Act. SLPs have additional and specific training and certification in speech and language topics. They work in school settings to help with facilitation of functional communication. Many things are pre-cursers to communication and the SLP knows the steps to take to help students communicate effectively. Even non-verbal students need to have appropriate ways to make their needs known.

The use of deep-breathing techniques, oral-motor training, group therapy, picture communication systems, and gesturing are all used by SLPs. Often times, the IEP may dictate that speech sessions are held in small groups. This is a wonderful way to work on communicating in a real-time functional setting. Bonds often form between students and confidence is built. This can be generalized to the classroom and at home.

SLPs and the treatment team may suggest visual schedules, use of pictures to help the student to communicate, assistive technology (AT) devices (such as DynaVox ® units or communication boards) to help accommodate the student's needs. Remember, these accommodations should be listed in the IEP or 504 plan and re-evaluated for appropriateness regularly.

Annual and short-term objectives for a student in speech include:

- Katrina will improve her language skills in ELA class as demonstrated by taking turns with a peer 80% of the time.
- Michael will improve text organization through use of graphic organizers to compose narratives in 4/5 opportunities.
- Tanisha will improve written expression for more effective participation in school.
- Max will stay on topic for x amount of turns with a peer.
- Marcie will use pronouns (I, we, his, etc.) in conversation 80% of the time.
- Jennifer will ask for assistance from the teacher when needed in 4/5 opportunities.
- Brant will re-tell a story with three or more details.
- Jason will use strategies for improved reading comprehension as evidenced by his ability to make predictions, answer comprehension questions, and demonstrate appropriate reading phrasing in 5/6 opportunities across three consecutive sessions.

Goals may include idioms, conversational skills, vocabulary, meeting basic needs in the classroom, and identifying emotions. Remember that school speech goals should relate to the school setting.

What Is a Physical Therapist?

Physical therapists are specifically trained in movement, muscles, functional performance, motor development, gross motor (large muscle group) function/ coordination, and positioning, among others. They are part of the "related services" category – part b in the Individuals with Disabilities Education Act.

Sometimes students have difficulty maneuvering in school. They may have disabilities which are physical, such as those causing decreased muscle tone, mitochondrial disease, and many others. Some students require the help of a skilled therapist to modify their environment to transfer (move) from one area to another. The physical therapist can help to adapt the environment for access. Providing safe lifting and positioning are critical for safety and to prevent injury. Additionally, students may need customized equipment or ways to move from the classroom to the lunch area. If there are steps to navigate, the physical therapist can assist with the safe performance of these tasks. Seating and positioning difficulties beyond what can be helped by the special education and school staff are often areas when a skilled therapist is called in for evaluation.

It's important to remember that the student's needs must be related to school issues and be provided in the most natural environment.

Goals need to be functional and can include the training of other staff members to assist the student or to modify the environment.

As with other therapists, reassessments and reviews must be done and notes will be taken each time the therapist works with the student or staff. Progress is documented and measured. Goals are written with frequency of services, location, duration, and 1:1 vs. consultative.

Annual and short-term goals for physical therapists may include:

- Mary will sit upright using an adaptive positioning device for 15 minutes 4/5 times during circle time as reported by the teacher.
- Patti will transfer from her chair to circle time independently 5/5 times according to data collected by Ms. Josephs.
- Nancy will navigate the hallway steps safely, without falling 100% of the time during transitions.

What Is a Related Service?

The IDEA states that related services can be any service that is developmental, corrective, and supportive. It includes any of the following: transportation, aides, language and speech, occupational or physical therapy, special strategies used for teaching, audiologists, social work, sign language, any supportive technological device, medical care, psychological assistance, recreation therapy, rehabilitative services/counseling, mobility, orientation services, and others. It is impossible to list every related service because every student is different, any service the student requires to meet her educational goals can be a related service. It is NOT appropriate for the school to state that they do not have funding for related service that the IEP team has deemed necessary.

Upon entering kindergarten, my son required the supervision of a Registered Nurse on a 1:1 basis throughout the school day. He also required a 1:1 aide. As a team, we discussed that it would be ridiculous to have two adults following him around all day. The nurse agreed to receive training on how to cue him appropriately, how to provide transition assistance, and in behavioral techniques. She agreed to perform these duties with consultation and training from various professionals (OTs, special educators, psychologists, and guidance staff). Of course, the school district was happy as they did not have to fund an additional aide!

The section of the IEP which contains the related services includes all of the ways the student's areas of weakness will be addressed. It should be detailed. Remember, that a goal that states, "Joshua will meet with the reading specialist weekly" is way too general. It's not measureable and is left open to interpretation of the reader. Here's an example of a better goal, "Joshua will meet for twenty minutes with the reading specialist two times per week." This is much better because no one can debate the meaning of the latter goal. Finally, the related services are generally calculated in minutes. An OT will be provided for 30 minutes weekly on a one to one basis in the occupational therapy room.

Chapter 2 Resources

www.alertprogram.com	Alert Program/How Does Your Engine Run?
www.aota.org	American Occupational Therapy Association
www.apta.org	American Physical Therapy Association
www.asha.org	American Speech-Language-Hearing Association
www.rtinetwork.org	Response to Intervention Network
www.pocketot.com	The Pocket Occupational Therapist

Chapter 3

Handwriting

One of the most common skills OTs work on in a school setting is handwriting. Problems with handwriting can occur in the general population as well as with children with special needs. While OTs are not handwriting teachers, we are able to assist students with the underlying difficulties that make up the task of writing. Handwriting does not simply involve the formation of letters and numbers, it also involves difficulty with the following: using the correct pressure on the pencil, the ability to grasp the pencil properly, cursive, staying within the lines of the paper, and spacing between words. Children need to develop handwriting skills as they progress through school and life but before the actual writing process begins, there are pre- writing skills that the student needs to learn and master.

What Are Some Warm Up Exercises for Writing?

There are many fun ways to warm up as a group prior to handwriting.

Out of the Pocket Activity

- Jumping jacks can be done in place.
- Various yoga poses are appropriate for the classroom.
- Call out a letter and ask students to try and form that letter using their bodies (similar to the YMCA dance).
- Do chair push-ups. With feet placed on the floor and both hands on sides of the seat, lift your body up slowly and hold for a few seconds. Slowly lower yourself back down. Don't help with your feet!
- Finger push-ups can be done at the desk. Place fingertips together. Bend and then straighten the fingers. Make sure the fingertips are always touching each other.
- Table push-ups can be done at the desk. Ensure feet are flat on the floor. Place the hands and forearms on the desk. Ask the student to lower his upper trunk down toward the desk and then use arms to push back into a seated position.
- Assign each student a small portion of putty or dough and place small items such as beads into the putty. Ask students to find them. Roll putty into a hot dog and use fingers to pinch the roll into smaller pieces. Form letters with the putty.
- Make circles with arms at shoulders, wrists, and thumbs. Start small and gradually increase the size of the circle. Reverse.
- Draw large figure eights with each arm ten times. The importance of the figure eight is that it requires students to cross their body's midline. This skill is an important one and can be adapted in many ways. Draw or tape a figure eight racetrack on the floor. Ask child to sit in the middle and roll cars along the entire track with the right arm. Repeat with left arm.

Use a large sheet of craft or poster paper and place on student's desk. Draw a "lazy 8 lying down."

- Ask students to give themselves a big hug for a job well done.

What Are the Skills Needed before Writing?

Often times, OTs work with children on their handwriting skills before they are expected to form letters. These skills are called "pre- writing" skills. Handwriting is a complex process because there are several areas of our body and brain that are used when writing. The cognitive (brain) abilities include: attention, visual-perceptual skills, interest in handwriting, and sequencing (first, then, last). The sensory motor-body awareness includes: posture and body control, motor planning, knowing right from left, crossing the body midline, and using both hands together. Handwriting also includes the ability to hold the pencil, scribble or mark on the paper, copy shapes, make "strokes" in all directions (vertical, horizontal, circular, and diagonal). As the student advances in school, copying from the board and from books makes the task more difficult as the skills required place more demands on the muscles of the hand, the eyes, and the attention required.

What Is Crossing the Midline?

A midline is an imaginary line in the middle of the body. When we are babies, we learn to bring our hands together and reach for toys with our hands while sitting on the floor. The ability for your student to cross her midline is extremely important for developing motor skills. It goes hand-in-hand with bilateral integration. As we develop, one of our hands becomes the dominant one and the other is the helper. If we do not develop a dominant hand, we do not refine the skills of either hand for writing, dressing, eating, and scissoring. When we read a page, our eyes must scan across the entire page. During writing, a student should be able to draw a horizontal line across the entire page with one hand and not switch hands in the middle. Many children prefer to use their right hand for activities on the right side of their body and their left hand for things on the left side of their body.

Many of my students demonstrate the lack of ability to cross their midline. Here's an example: A student in pre-school is observed during snack time. The juice box is on the left side of his placemat and the graham crackers are on the right side of the placemat. You observe that he uses his left hand only to pick up the juice box and his right hand only to pick up and eat the crackers. He does not change how he's reaching for items during the entire snack time. You encourage him to try to pick up the juice box with his right hand and you notice distress when he tries. You may need to provide encouragement for your student to cross his hands across his body. Have fun with the activities listed below and be sure to ask your student not to move his body (trunk) side to side, but instead have his arms move to cross the imaginary line across the center of his body.

OUT OF THE POCKET ACTIVITY

- Use a large poster board or butcher paper and encourage the student to stand at the middle of her desk and take turns using each arm to fill the opposite half with shapes and colors.
- Ask students to lay prone (tummy down) on a carpeted area and complete their written work or complete a game or puzzle. This will require them to cross over the board to move and arrange the pieces.
- Students can pass a beach ball back and forth. Put on some music, move chairs next to each other, and make a chain of friends and pass the ball in one direction. Switch directions when you stop the music. This can

even be done while students are standing at their desks.

- Sit back to back and pass a ball around your body to each other. My students love doing this to fun, bouncy music.
- Scrub down a chalk board or use a sponge to clean large windows together. Hold the sponge or brush with both hands.
- Work on paper/pencil activities such as matching the doggie to his bone. Draw the doggie on the left side of the paper and the bone on the right side of the paper. Make sure your student doesn't move the paper while drawing the line, but instead moves his pencil across the paper. You can draw anything you want that may go together and interests your student. Mazes, word searches, and tracing are other paper/pencil activities you can try.
- Using a large whiteboard or chalk board, draw a figure eight lying on its side (like the infinity sign). Draw a rainbow with many colors. Have your student stand in the middle of the shape and trace the shape back and forth. Encourage him to cross his arm across his body while completing the activity.
- Use colorful pieces of fabric to write numbers or letters in the air and across their bodies.

What Is Bilateral Integration?

Bilateral means both sides and integration means working together. Bilateral integration is when both sides of the body work together to complete a task. Often, the hands are completing different tasks to accomplish a common goal. There is awareness of sides, right and left. Generally, one side is dominant and the other is used as a stabilizer. When a student has difficulty in this area, she may avoid crossing her midline. This means that she may not be able to coordinate her hands together to complete a task. She may have difficulty with scissoring since it requires one hand to cut while the other stabilizes the paper. A student with poor bilateral integration may also have trouble with lacing shoes, jumping jacks, bicycle riding, and threading beads. Sometimes a student may appear "clumsy" and may have a great deal of frustration. Many of my clients have difficulty cutting meats with a fork and knife. This task requires both hands to work together.

Children with bilateral integration difficulty should be given motivating tasks that are specifically planned to be fun. Encourage wording such as "use both hands" or "use your helper hand."

- Cut worksheets into halves or quarters and ask students to crawl around the room to find the pieces.
- Set up a bakery center and use the hands together to roll, pat, and create pastries out of real or play dough.
- Complete jumping jacks, skip, or do "scissors" by crossing legs over each other when lying on the back.
- Scooter activities in the gym use the entire body.
- Shuffle cards and play card games which require the student to hold the cards in one hand and pick up with the other.
- Provide containers of different sizes to practice opening and closing, place a treat in each one for a fun surprise!
- String beads of different shapes and sizes.
- Use different veggies to stamp onto paper. The dominant hand is the primary one, but the helper hand is needed to stabilize the paper and ink container.
- Squeeze sponges of different shapes. Use colored water for more fun.
- Play hide and seek with various shaped items in putty or dough.
- Tearing paper is a fun activity. Use paper to make a craft.
- Origami uses both hands and is fun.
- Set up a t-ball area at recess or gym and encourage use of both arms to swing at the ball.

- Work on classroom exercises prior to longer lessons. Encourage students to clasp fingers on both hands and move arms across the body in circles—big and small; diagonally; etc. Move to music for relaxation. (Neck rolls are an extra way to relax!)

What Is Vision?

Vision is the ability to see with our eyes. However, we need to make sense of what we've seen. We don't usually consider that our eyes must work together to focus: they must move to see what's around us; help us to see objects near and far; and they must be able to determine details of what we are looking at. When we have processed all of those things, we can then use our hands together with the information from our eyes to complete a task. Most children have an evaluation of their eyesight performed by an ophthalmologist to rule out problems with vision or have a screening at school. The doctor will use charts with either pictures or letters, examine the eyes with various ophthalmic instruments, and complete tests to look at the structures of the eye. It is at this time glasses may be recommended. Additionally, when a child has headaches, developmental delays, and difficulty in school; I always recommend a functional vision assessment by a developmental (sometimes called a behavioral) optometrist. There can be difficulties not only with visual acuity, but also in the processing of the information we receive via our eyes.

See "Visual Supports" section for more details and for visual accommodations.

What Is Hand-Eye Coordination?

Hand-eye coordination is when the visual system and brain give information to the hands to complete movements necessary to successfully complete tasks such as painting, writing, and catching a ball. Additionally, this skill is used in gross motor movements. When a student plays baseball, he must be able to see the ball coming toward him to either hit or catch it. The eyes and body need to work together so functional activities can be done. It is important to remember that the eyes, hands, and arms make constant small adjustments to ensure that the activity is done successfully. Here are some activities that you can do to work on hand-eye coordination:

- Hang a Koosh or tennis ball from a string on a small hook either in the garage, ceiling, or a doorjamb and have your student use arms individually and then together to hit the ball.
- Encourage your student to lie on his back as you hold the ball on the string. Ask him to hit the ball with the arm(s) you name (left, right, and together).
- While lying on his back, your student can toss the ball up into the air. Therapy catalogues or even discount stores offer balls with many different textures and colors for more variety. Beach balls are slower moving and larger for beginners.
- Build a small tower with blocks and then knock it down for fun!
- Sit on the ground facing each other and roll balls of various sizes to each other.
- Copy shapes or trace them using differently sized puzzle pieces or blocks.
- Pour water with different sized cups.
- Play balloon volleyball.

Sports such as tennis, badminton, and softball can be great for working on hand-eye coordination, but be careful not to place your student into a competitive setting when he has not mastered this skill.

What Are Posture, Positioning, and Core Muscles?

Without a good base of support, a student may have difficulty with prolonged use of the arms and legs. Let's think about a student in school all day. She must sit at her desk for long periods of time. If she has a weak core, she may begin her day sitting upright in her chair, but as time passes she fatigues quickly and begins to slump onto her desk. When she must complete paper and pencil tasks, she is already tired and lacks the energy to use her arms. I encourage you to attempt to write a paragraph while slumped over at your desk; it is truly difficult. Humans need a good strong base of support in our trunk to complete tasks with our arms and hands. The core muscles support the shoulder muscles, which support the arm muscles, which support the hand musculature—it's like a pyramid that needs a strong base.

If the base is weak, then the rest crumbles immediately or can only support the top for a brief period. You can ask your student's teacher about her posture at her desk or notice her posture during homework time in the evening. Also, do your own "assessment" and ask her to write a paragraph in her best handwriting and take note of her body position, writing at the beginning and end of the assignment.

I once interviewed a school OT and she stated that the first person in the school she makes it a point to meet is the custodian. She further explained that he/she would be the person in charge of moving and adapting the furniture in the classroom for her students. I have since made it a practice to do the same!

It is extremely important to make sure that a student is seated in a chair that is fitted to his specific size. In order to complete fine motor or skilled tasks involving the hands, we need a base of support. Our core muscles provide the base of support we need to be successful while using our hands. Positioning with the feet flat on the floor is important while completing seated tasks. We should sit in our chairs with our thighs parallel to the floor, our back should be comfortably resting vertically on the chair, and our forearms should be resting on the table parallel to the floor. We call this a 90-90-90 position. The result is a 90 degree angle at our ankles, knees, elbows, and at our hips. If a student is slouching in his chair, he will quickly fatigue when using his hands.

- Try it! Adjust your chair so that your body is not in the proper position, such as feet not reaching the floor or adjust your seat too low. Now, see how much work you can accomplish comfortably. Working at a desk or having a chair that is in the incorrect position causes fatigue or a decrease in the ability to focus.

- To further modify the student's writing surface, you can do the following:
  - ✓ To help with positioning of the wrist and hands at the table during handwriting, an inclined surface works well. Use a three ring binder that's four inches wide. Place the paper on a clip board on top of the binder. The use of the binder provides an inclined surface which helps with positioning of the hand and wrist for handwriting.
  - ✓ Your student should be permitted to rest his forearms on the table for greater stability when using his fingers.
  - ✓ A clip board can be used to ensure the paper does not slide around on the desk. Sometimes, children have difficulty holding the paper with the hand opposite the writing hand. Therapists call the non-dominant hand the "helper hand."
  - ✓ Writers using their left hand must have their feet on the floor as above, however their paper should be placed in front of their left shoulder. Additionally, their paper can be turned to a forty-five degree angle. It is important to monitor the posture of students using their left hand as they may develop issues with positioning which can later cause fatigue.

What Is a Web Space and Thumb Opposition and What Do They Have to Do with Writing?

Before I became a pediatric therapist, I worked with patients who had injuries to their hands. The ability to use our hands functionally is critical to success in our daily lives.

Yes, when illness and disability forces us, we can adapt and accommodate, but things will probably be much more difficult. Our thumbs are used constantly for various tasks. I bet you probably don't even realize how important our thumbs are to us every day. A thumb allows us to grasp and turn a key or doorknob. Thumbs are used to hold our pens, toothbrushes, and toilet paper! Make the OK sign with your hand. The circular space between your thumb and index finger is called the "web space." It is called that because the area is webbed-like a duck's feet. The ability to use the tips of our fingers allows us to make small (fine) motor adjustments and decreases the overall fatigue (tiredness) of the muscles of the hand and arm.

Did you know that the muscles of the hand are unique because some are fully contained in the hand (intrinsic), but some are long enough to attach to the bones of the forearm (extrinsic)? It is important to fully understand how our bodies are formed to ensure that the hand functions well. The thumb has the most muscles of all of the fingers (yet it's the shortest). Thumbs are able to move in all different ways. As children develop, they learn to use their thumbs to pick smaller items up and then progress toward using thumbs to "face" the other fingers. Therapists call this task "opposition." Try to use your thumb to touch the tips of all of the other fingers in order. This task is called "serial opposition." It's necessary to use this motion to grasp and hold on to the writing utensil.

OUT OF THE POCKET ACTIVITY

- Cut a small area out of the bottom of a sock to ensure that only the thumb, index, and middle fingers are exposed. It's a great visual and physical cue to help students to isolate the fingers used for the appropriate grip on the pencil.
- The tennis ball is one of my favorite therapy tools and by cutting a slit in

the side, make a "mouth" and with one hand, ask the student to squeeze the ball to "open the mouth" and the other hand to "feed" the mouth. Put google eyes or use markers to draw facial features on the ball for a more realistic experience.

- Use any kind of dropper-including turkey basters and eye droppers to squeeze and transfer water from one container to another. Use food coloring to make this more fun.

- Theraputty or home-made dough is great when placed into the hand and squeezed. Encourage kids to hold the putty in their palms while using their thumbs to dig in and make holes. This could be done at the desk as a quiet activity while other students are still working.

- Geoboards can be purchased on-line, from teacher stores, or even made with a wooden block and nails. Stretch rubber bands over the pegs to make different shapes.

- Any game such as chess and checkers where items are picked up between the thumb and first two fingers works on web-space development. Connect Four is another great game.

- Clothes pins are great for working on many fine motor tasks and can be painted to match paint sample cards (found at home improvement stores). You can write upper or lower case letters, multiplication facts, and more on the clothes pin and ask students to clip them onto their match. Hanging up items in the classroom onto a clothesline would be a great activity for students with handwriting goals in the IEP.

- Tearing paper vs. cutting at the craft center would be a wonderful way to work on hand-coordination.

- Tweezers of any size to pick up items can be used for centers.

- Triangular pencils and crayons are great for younger students.
- Use of chopsticks vs. fork/spoon is a fun way to build up the hand and thumb muscles for coordination.

Teach Me about Different Ways to Hold a Pencil.
Why is My Student Not Able to Use a Tripod Grasp?

The way a student holds a pencil is important because the muscles used for grip can fatigue when over-used or used in ways other than for which they were designed. There are many functional grasps. Here are a few examples:

- How do you hold your purse straps, shopping bag, or briefcase handle? It's called a hook grasp and the fingers do the work, leaving the thumb out.
- When you hold your key, a lateral pinch grasp is used.
- Grasp a large glass of water and you're using the thumb and fingers to wrap around the glass.

The grasp a student uses on the pencil is important because with the tripod grasp, the student can write at a reasonable speed without fatigue on his muscles. Your student may be using a stable grasp. This means that she may be using all of the muscles that she can to stabilize her hand while writing due to weak muscles. She may be placing all of her fingers on the pencil for extra stability. When a muscle or groups of muscles are weak, our bodies use a strategy called "compensation." Compensation means that we try to use other muscles or different movements to make up for a weakness. It is important to encourage fun activities which are strategically designed to work on strengthening her thumb, pointer, and middle finger. The more practice she has using them together, the better able she will be to complete a tripod grasp. It is important not to force a student to use a tripod grasp before she is ready to do so. Keep the activities short and fun for maximal interest and participation.

Out of the Pocket Activity

- Break student crayons in half so that there is a smaller surface area on which to place fingers. Use a golf pencil with an eraser placed on top as a smaller pencil.

- Encourage students to work with putty or dough to find small craft beads or coins.

- Bowl by setting up erasers like bowling pins. Use fingertips to roll a marble as the ball.

- Cut a slit into the top of containers. Place small items into the slit like colored paper clips, coins, and small pegs. Work on counting with the items or sort them by twos, tens, etc.

- Tear small pieces of tissue paper up and use fingers to roll them up and glue them onto a piece of construction paper to make patterns.

- Use tweezers to pick small items up. Therapy catalogues have fun colored and shaped tweezers that kids love.

- Use an inclined surface while writing and doing crafts. A chalk or white board that can bevel is a super idea for writing. A student is much more likely to use the proper wrist and hand motions while using an angled surface on which to work.

- For the desktop, use a three ring binder that's two inches wide. Place a piece of paper on a clip board on top of the binder so that the student may turn it to a comfortable angle. The use of the binder provides an inclined surface which helps with positioning of the hand and wrist for handwriting.

- Use small stampers of different shapes. It's fun to correlate the stamps with the upcoming holiday. Sometimes, dollar stores carry stampers for a low price around the season or holiday.

- Perler beads come in all different colors. Picking up such a small bead is wonderful for developing fine motor skills.
- Paint with Q-tips®.

Are We Ready for Writing Letters Yet?

No! We need to talk about a few more skills that are critical to master before we teach writing of letters and numbers. Every letter is made up of different "strokes" or lines we make on the paper. As typical children grow, there is a predictable pattern in which these strokes develop. When we have a student with special needs, the strokes may not develop at the proper age and/or in the proper order. Children are simply not ready to write if they have not mastered the strokes for

Approximate Age of Student	Handwriting Stroke Mastery
By one year of age	Holds crayon and may crumple paper up.
By two years of age	Scribbles on the paper and may be able to imitate by scribbling in a circle, side to side (horizontal) or up and down (vertical) direction.
By three years of age	Imitates a horizontal and vertical line. Imitates a circle.
By four years of age	Copies a horizontal and vertical line. Copies a circle, imitates a cross, imitates a right/left diagonal, and imitates a square.
By five years of age	Copies a cross, a right and left diagonal, imitates a triangle and X.
By six years of age	Copies an X, copies a triangle, and can draw a "big" or "small" line.

writing. Occupational therapists assess the student's readiness for writing by using several formal or standardized assessments. Most look at the student's ability to form the strokes of pre-writing by a pre-determined age. The following is a chart of the typical development therapists look for.

If a student cannot recognize any of the pre-writing strokes and further, if they cannot form the individual strokes; it is inappropriate to teach the formation of letters and numbers. When broken down, every letter is composed of one of the basic strokes. I encourage you to analyze the letters in print of the alphabet and identify which pre-writing strokes the letter is made of. The correct formation of the pre-writing strokes will lead to neater handwriting in print. The same is true for cursive letters. There are a few pre-strokes that need to be learned in order to form the letters. Note, there are many different ways to teach both print and cursive writing. Also, every school district may use a different form of accepted writing curriculum.

Teachers and therapists have many different methods of teaching handwriting. Overall, the same techniques are followed to ensure students become good and confident writers.

1. Demonstrate the proper formation of the strokes to the student in the order that they are developmentally learned. Go back to the last stroke that the student has mastered and then move forward to the next one. For example, if the student correctly copies a horizontal line but not a diagonal line, practice both horizontal and vertical lines to build up confidence and then continually work on diagonal lines. It is best to move on to drawing X after single diagonal line is mastered.
   - Use different "mediums" for practicing the pre-writing strokes such as: shaving cream, writing in dough, pudding, and sand.
   - Use stickers to form lines and ask students to trace between the stickers.

- Make strokes on vertical surfaces to encourage wrist movement.
- Use different utensils such as chalk, paint, crayons, and vibrating pens.
- Trace shapes with index finger on items such as sand paper for sensory feedback. Use puffy paint or glue for texture and to add interest.
- Use foam pieces of different colors to make the basic pre-writing strokes and allow students to choose the correct stroke as you call it out.
- Encourage students to trace shapes in the air or find shapes of objects in the classroom and identify their shapes.
- Say the names of the strokes as you teach them.

2. Move to paper/pencil work. Make sure positioning of the desk and chair are correct for the student's height. As students draw, use self and/or peer-evaluation to check each other's work. Learning to evaluate your own writing will be critical as writing gets increasingly difficult.

3. Make sure the student knows his left from his right. When teaching writing and strokes, begin with instruction to start writing on the left side of the paper. Knowing top vs. bottom is also important.

4. Add a designated area such as a box or lines that the student should write inside of. Giving borders early on will encourage students to recognize and further control the size of their writing.

Out of the Pocket Activity

What Are Some Pre-Writing Group Activities Appropriate for the Classroom?

- Use the electronic board or overhead projector to write a shape and ask students to write it in the air or copy onto paper.
- Draw a stick person together. If students are able to add more detail, encourage them to do so.

- Fill pencil boxes with sand, rice, or other sensory material. Ask them to use their fingers or pencils to draw a shape you name in their own "sensory box."
- Use music and ask students to scribble or draw to the "feeling" or beat of the music.
- Place a large sheet of paper on the board. Ask students to add shapes to the paper making an abstract art picture.
- Ask students to draw shapes on a partner's back using their index finger. Add letters and numbers later on.
- Play "Simon Says," but give commands such as "Simon Says make a diagonal line," or "Simon Says make a big circle with your left hand."
- Call out directions such as, "with your green crayon, make a circle on the paper." This activity can be adapted for older students as follows, "with your red pen, make a letter x on the top, right side of your paper." Adding more steps to any task will always make it more difficult to follow, and works on attention and multi-step commands.

Writing Letters

Whatever the curriculum you use, writing letters is important to our communication as a society. There continues to be a debate as to whether or not to teach handwriting as technology evolves. When OTs and teachers receive an IEP goal for handwriting, it is our legal responsibility to work on that goal. Different therapists use different methods to teach letters and numbers. Many school districts are adopting the Handwriting Without Tears® Method. It is important for teachers and parents to communicate about the specific curriculum being taught for writing. The child should have consistency between the two settings. Most teachers would be willing to provide extra copies of the worksheets for additional practice at home.

When forming letters with my students, I always identify with my students the basic pre-writing shapes that form that letter. For this reason, I (and many others) teach the letters not in alphabetical order, but in the order in which the basic strokes are learned. Here's an example: I would introduce H before A. This is because the letter H has horizontal and vertical strokes. The letter O is taught prior to letter Q as the latter has a diagonal component. Lower case letters are much the same. The letter t in print is much simpler to form than the letter x for a student who has difficulty with diagonal strokes. I teach the lower case letters first which look like their upper case partners. For example, P looks the same as p and o looks the same as O.

See the ideas in the previous section for pre-writing skills as they may be duplicated for forming letters. It is always best to use a multi- sensory approach to teaching any new skill. Use different mediums in which to write letters such as: in sand, with shaving cream. Form them with foods such as raisins, with pebbles, and other small items. Please remember that it's critical to show the student how you form the letter or pre-writing strokes. Watching a good model is a great way to learn.

 OUT OF THE POCKET ACTIVITY

- Always practice writing numbers and letters on lines or within defined spaces. It will be more difficult to transition from blank paper in the lower grades to handwriting paper later on.
- Play with letters and numbers as much as possible.
- When reading to the class, point out different letters that you are working on. Copy a page from the reading book and ask all students to circle the letters that you request. This can be done as a group or as a center activity.

- Place writing paper over sandpaper, plastic sheets (used for needlepoint), or foam sheets to add sensory interest.
- Fill pencil boxes with sand, rice, or other sensory material. Ask them to use their fingers or pencils to draw a shape you name in their own "sensory box."
- Ask students to write letters on each other's backs while waiting in line for bathroom time or specials.
- Draw hop-scotch with sidewalk chalk and ask students to jump on specific letters. This could work in the classroom by placing large puzzle foam mats on the ground and writing letters on each one. Call a letter and ask the student to stand on it.
- If there's a trampoline handy, the same could be done by drawing letters with sidewalk chalk on the trampoline's surface.
- Remember that if a student cannot identify the letter correctly, he will not be able to write it correctly without a model when asked to do so.

How Do I Work on Spacing between Words and Margins?

It's critical to monitor the spacing between younger students' words. When beginning sentences, reiterate the importance of making a space so that sentences are legible. When spacing is an issue, there are several tricks and tips therapists use. Placing a visual reminder at the top of the student's desk is an excellent way to help them to remember what to do instead of the teacher standing over their shoulder or verbally reminding them. Most children with autism, for example, are visual learners and do much better with a visual reminder on their desk or paper. For example: Laminate a piece of paper with a properly spaced sentence and the technique you choose from the list below to remediate the spacing (such as the method with stickers).

- Use a tongue depressor or craft stick to demonstrate how spacing should look. I encourage every student to decorate his "space man" or "space dude" (older students) in whatever manner they choose. Individualizing the tool is important to ensure the student is willing to use it.

- Use the index and middle fingers together to make the space between words. This technique is difficult for students who are left handed as they must cross over the left hand to make the space. I generally encourage them to use the "space dude" technique.

- Graph paper is an accommodation that is common in IEPs for both spacing and math. It's a great visual way to organize sentences when learning about spacing.

- Place a few stickers of stop signs or red on the right margin and stickers that are green, such as smiley faces on the left side.

- LegiGuide® paper (see photo) helps students with size and spacing and was created by an OT. Photo courtesy of LegiGuide.com.

- Many therapists use stickers between words. When the student is writing, he could place stickers on the paper between words or when he is finished with the writing, he could check his work by making sure that the stickers can fit between the words. It's a wonderful thing when students can self-monitor.

- FOR MARGINS: Use a highlighter on the left margin so that students can remember to go back to that side to continue a sentence instead of cramming near the end of the line.

- Use a green marker to mark the left margin for "GO" and a red marker to mark the right margin for "STOP."

- Ask students to draw a light circle between words so that handwriting is not interrupted with placing an item between words. As students get used to the spacing, ask students to mentally visualize the circles vs. actually drawing them.
- When all else fails, use a food reward such as Smarties ® candy or an M&M® between words.

What if My Student Presses Too Hard on the Pencil and It Breaks?

Some students have difficulty grading their pressure on the writing utensil. This may be due to a difficulty grading or determining exactly how much pressure is needed. Sometimes children write quickly just to get the information down on the paper. If students are frequently breaking the lead in their pencil, there are a few things that can be done.

Out of the Pocket activity

- Try using a mechanical pencil for writing practice. When the student presses too hard, the lead breaks.
- Place something such as a piece of sand paper or a few sheets of construction paper underneath the writing paper. This will cause a hole or indentation on the paper when pressing too hard.
- If it's age appropriate, use an erasable pen to alleviate the use of pencils altogether.
- Practice coloring with pencils to make various shades of gray. Also, practice with colored pencils.
- What if my student presses too lightly on the paper?

- Use carbon paper, this forces students to press harder to reach all of the layers of paper.
- Use #1 pencil as the lead is darker.
- Make tracings of different leaves and objects.
- Use a weighted pencil or create one yourself using metal nuts that fit around the pencil.
- Try using a pencil gripper. If you live near a teacher store, they can be found there. If not, most catalogues for children with special needs offer packs of different grippers. There's no "universal" gripper, try out different ones to see which works best for your student.

How Do I Help with Letters That Are Too Big or Small? How Do I Help with Letter Reversals?

Handwriting deficits include difficulty writing letters that are the appropriate size (letter size differentiation). It is extremely difficult to read words composed of letters that are mixed big and small. When students are in higher grades and have formed "bad" habits, they become more interested in simply getting the information down on their paper and lose sight of legibility. Sometimes, it is not at all practical for therapists/teachers to work on sizing of letters due to many other issues that more significantly impact their learning.

I want to make sure to reiterate that it is extremely important to begin writing letters and numbers on lined paper. Bad habits form quickly, so it's best to ensure that they not start in the first place. Visual-spatial elements include the lines that are present to help ensure legibility. The middle line is often dotted in primary paper, and the bottom line is generally called the baseline.

Out of the Pocket Activity

- There are several writing papers that can now be purchased at discount stores. Some have the bottom space (between the baseline and the middle line) highlighted with yellow or pink. Students keep their lower case letters (except for taller letters such as t and f) in the colored space.
- The actual lines can be highlighted with different colored markers.
- Raised line paper can be purchased so that a sensory component is added.
- Make your own raised lined paper with Wikki Sticks ® by sticking them on the top line for example. When the student's line physically bumps the stick, he receives physical feedback. This method is not at all practical for students who are jotting quick notes down, but is a great method to use when teaching letters or working specifically one on one.
- Use glitter or regular glue to trace the baseline. When it dries, it creates a great texture for helping students "feel' and "bump" the baseline. (Do the same for any line on the paper.)
- Use graph paper to keep letters organized and neatly in each box.
- Cut a section out of a large index card which will only show the line of paper that the student is writing on. Some students can become overwhelmed by the view of the entire paper at once.
- Ask students to make groups of letters that are "tall" such as t and f; letters that drop or "dig" below the line such as "g and p"; short letters a, m, c. Grouping the letters and using words that are fun and apply to a student's specific interests allow for better learning and then generalization of skills.
- When teaching students the concepts of tall, mid-height, and letters that dip below the lines, adding a gross motor activity is a great idea. For

example, yell out the letter "b" and then place arms straight up into the air. Yell letter "a" and students place hands on hips. For letter "y" arms go straight down to the student's side. This would look a bit like a cheerleader practice. Any time you add a gross motor (large body movements) to an activity, an entirely new memory or connection is made for the student.

Another one of the most frequent IEP goals I work on are those dealing with letter reversals. The following letters are commonly reversed: b/d, s, q/p/g, j, f, and m/w. Numbers may represent totally different codes when switched or reversed. Students commonly reverse letters in kindergarten and first grade, however if the student is still reversing letters by age seven or eight (through second grade), special intervention may be necessary. Children with learning disabilities can reverse letters, however many students with and without special needs commonly need help with reversals.

Some children who reverse letters may have visual-perceptual issues and difficulty with knowing their right from their left, this is called right/left discrimination. Teachers and therapists can easily help students with this skill.

OUT OF THE POCKET ACTIVITY

- Encourage games such as Simon Says or the Hokey Pokey to learn left and right.
- Place your arms out in front of you with palms facing away from your body. Now, spread your thumb out from the first finger.
- The left hand naturally makes a letter "L."
- If you make a fist with each hand and point your thumb up toward the sky, the left hand forms letter b and right hand forms letter d.

- Ask students to wear a wrist band or small bracelet when writing to denote their left hand.
- Play the game, "Left, Center, Right®." It's a fun dice game that can be purchased anywhere and can be played in a therapy session or with a small group of students. (Adds the physical or kinesthetic learning component.)
- Place a large letter "L" on the left side of the classroom and an "R" for the right. The same can be done on the student's desk and/or paper for easy reference.
- Place a sticker on the right or left side of the desk.
- Arrange things in a sequence starting left to right and vice versa.
- Lower case "b" looks like a baseball bat with a ball in front of it. Lower case "d" looks like a drum with a taller drumstick next to it or like a dog with his tail up to the right. Anytime you can add a visual representation to a letter, it is more likely to be meaningful to the student. Be creative and ask the student for ideas.
- Use multi-sensory techniques to work on letters. Use different "mediums" for practicing the pre-writing strokes such as: shaving cream, writing in dough, pudding, and sand.
- Keep a model of correctly formed letters on the student's desk. Use a visual next to the letter to ensure that the student can identify it. For example, place a baseball bat picture with the letter b; a picture of a dog with letter d, etc.
- Try using colors to code letters which are commonly reversed. Letters with the loop or hook on the right, such as p, b, r, h are highlighted in blue. Letters a, d, j, q are coded in pink. Let students choose the colors and their meaning so that they will remember them. Tape an index card on the top of the desk.

- Over teach only one letter at a time. Work only on "b" until the student masters it.
- Ask the student to circle a letter he commonly reverses in a story or a worksheet.
- Remember that if a student cannot identify the letter correctly, he will not be able to write it correctly when asked to.

How Do I Teach Cursive?

According to today's common core standards, cursive may be abandoned in lieu of keyboarding instruction. With the advancement of technology comes the hot topic of whether or not to teach cursive to today's students. It is believed that cursive writing can contribute to increased hand-eye coordination, motor skills, and boost academic achievement. For instructional purposes, I have included this section to assist teachers, therapists, and students in helping students with the basic principles of cursive writing.

As with print, every school district (or teacher) adopts a cursive handwriting curriculum. There are basic strokes in cursive writing that must be mastered. The Handwriting Without Tears Program ® teaches handwriting in a vertical fashion as the creator feels that this makes the transition between print and cursive easier. Other programs teach cursive on a slant. It is strongly encouraged that you speak with the child's teacher to determine how and if/when cursive will be taught and further, obtain worksheets to practice at home. The same ideas listed in the previous section "writing letters" will pertain to both print and cursive. Please remember that it's critical to show the student how you form the letter or pre-writing strokes. Watching a good model is a great way to learn.

The key factor in success with any writing is that the student is able to correctly identify the letters when presented randomly. I recommend cutting out cursive letters from worksheets provided by the school and then play various games with them. One of my favorites is to call out a letter and ask the student to place the letter on something that starts with it. Then, practice writing that letter.

Some programs for handwriting include: Handwriting Without Tears, Zaner-Bloser, Loops and Other Groups, and Size Matters Handwriting Program.

Special Consideration for Children Who Are Left-Handed

Children who write with their left hand should not be criticized or looked at as "different." The use of their left hand is no more a choice than you had to use your right hand! When left-handed students write, their hand drags across the letters they have already written, which may cause a smearing.

- Use a fine point marker or felt-tip pen to decrease smudging.
- When teaching writing, model the formation of the letter and task with your left hand.
- Encourage the student to turn the paper (30 degrees clockwise) instead of adapting his grip or arm position—which may cause the development of bad habits causing increased fatigue to the muscles of the hand and arm.
- Allow for modifications of worksheets and lists so that the student can place words in the right margin.
- Position students so that they are not bumping arms with their right-handed classmates.
- Allow students to use modified notebooks, it can be frustrating (even painful) when the student's arm is constantly on the metal rings binding the notebook.
- There are a few stores on-line for left-handed products:
  - www.anythingleft-handed.co.uk
  - www.lefthandedworld.com
  - www.therapyshoppe.com

How Can I Help My Students to Be More Responsible for Their Own Writing?

The chart on the next page is a great graphic organizer that I created for my students. We exchange papers with a friend or allow students to self-check. It can be adapted for students by adding: smiling and frowning faces; with a scoring system; signs such as those pictured below; or a simple yes/no column. Note that the last row, "I used vivid, colorful words and descriptions in my story" is for older students. I wanted to include it as an example for higher level writing.

Proofreading Chart

Name:		Partner:	
I used my neatest handwriting.			
My sentences begin with a capital letter.			
I used capital letters when I was supposed to.			
My sentences end with a period, question mark, or exclamation point.			
I did my best at spelling words correctly.			
I used vivid, colorful words and descriptions in my story.			

Chapter 3 Resources

www.anythinglefthanded.co.uk	Anything Left Handed
www.hwtears.com	Handwriting Without Tears
www.lefthandedworld.net	Lefthanded World
www.LegiGuide.com	LegiGuide Writing Paper
www.realotsolutions.com	Size Matters Handwriting Program
www.therapyshoppe.com	Therapy Shoppe
www.therapro.com	Therapro (Loops and Other Groups) and Drive-Through Menus
www.zaner-bloser.com	Zaner-Bloser

Chapter 4

Fine Motor in the Classroom

Fine motor skills involve the use of the muscles of the hand. Some of the muscles originate and then attach in the palm and fingers. Others are actually located in the forearm and send tendons down to the fingers and thumb. The process of using your hands for any fine motor task involves the stable base of support of your body. Think of the body and core muscles as the bottom of the pyramid. A strong core/base is the foundation of stability. When there are any problems with fine motor skills, consider issues with not just the hands but also the student's posture/core muscles; strength of the entire arm; visual-perceptual deficits; and motivation.

Where Do I Begin Working on Fine Motor Skills?

To work on fine motor skills, begin with any activity in which the student has to use his arm muscles to bear the weight of his body (this is called weight-bearing). Crawling through obstacle courses, walking like various animals, lying tummy down on the floor, and propping the body up by the arms while in circle time are all activities you can try for weight bearing. A child who has missed the crawling stage may also need to work on additional weight bearing tasks.

The student's arm strength overall needs to be increased in order to work on those smaller hand muscles. Try using monkey bars on the playground, playing team games such as tug-of-war, using large therapy bands for exercise. Climbing up on rock walls or other gym equipment can be done without drawing specific attention to the student with weak arms. Remember when beginning, start slowly and make sure that the student experiences success to build confidence.

Next, look at the student's ability to use both arms together for functional tasks. Read bilateral integration in my first book, The Pocket Occupational Therapist for Caregivers of Children with Autism and Special Needs (Jessica Kingsley Publishers, 2013), for more ideas on this topic.

What Can I Do in My Classroom to Work on Fine Motor Skills?

Fine motor tasks are easily worked on in the classroom with a little creativity! The activities listed below can be done with the entire classroom to avoid isolation and calling attention to the student with fine motor coordination difficulties. If an activity is too difficult for the student, use a larger item instead so that it's easier to grasp.

OUT OF THE POCKET ACTIVITY

- Opening and closing containers of different shapes and sizes can be fun. Work on classification of objects by placing them into the various containers.
- Use hole paper punches. Punch with different colored paper and use the punches to decorate or for educational crafts at center time.
- Play with dough or clay to create items related to the curriculum.
- Save old greeting cards and punch holes out of them in a pattern

matching the picture. Allow students to lace through the holes.

- Use paper clips to make necklaces in different patterns.
- Marbles can be used in many different ways, for example: use a spoon to move marbles from container to container; and/or place marbles on top of golf tees which are affixed to a block of Styrofoam.
- Buttons of different shapes and sizes can be strung, glued for crafts, and sorted.
- Straws can be placed into containers whose lids have been hole punched.
- Stickers with letters, shapes, and numbers can be placed onto paper with matching stickers.
- Write letters on clothes pins and ask students to clip onto index cards with matching letters. Try this with cursive/print letters, upper/lower case letters, math problems/answers, etc. The potential is unlimited! This can be done with colors and paint chips too.
- Paint with tiny sponges.
- Use stampers with and without handles.
- Form various shapes, letters, and numbers with pipe cleaners.
- Pom-poms can be sorted by shape, size, and color.
- Tearing paper, magazines, and thin fabric.
- Tweezers can be purchased in various shapes and colors OR use tongs from the kitchen store for smaller produce to pick up items.
- Manipulate parquetry to form different shapes.
- Work puzzles of all shapes and sizes.
- Geoboards and rubber bands are excellent for strengthening both fine motor and visual perceptual skills.
- Legos can be set up so that the student has to imitate a specific pattern or shape.
- Pick-up sticks are always fun.

- Use stencils to trace shapes, letters, and numbers.
- Dominoes can be awesome for fine-motor and team building!
- Use of iPads, keyboards, and other technology requires use of individual and groups of finger muscles.

The activities listed above can be adapted for each student's specific needs and to your lesson plans.

Ideas for Group Fine Motor Muscle Warm-Up Exercises

It's always fun to work as a class to warm up muscles and get ready for difficult work. Students can watch and model each other's movement and no one is isolated. Use of music and rhythm can be organizing and add fun and relaxation to any warm-up activity.

The class' hands may be tired from writing longer assignments or essays. Often, children with special needs or speech delays have difficulty expressing their feelings and may not even realize that their hand muscles are fatigued and they need some TLC. Having been a therapist who has worked in the area of hand therapy, this is true for children and grown-ups alike.

- Use each hand to massage the palms of the other in a circular motion. Move to the fingers and up the forearm. It's great to add scented lotion choices if children are not especially sensitive to scents.
- Ask students to place their palms together with elbows resting on the desk. Now slowly slide the elbows away from each other, but keep palms together. This is a great stretch! Now, slowly bring elbows back together. Repeat at least 10 times each.
- Clapping hands to a beat can invigorate muscles.
- Finger plays are fun for younger children. Even pretending hands are "talking" to each other is fun. Finger puppets can be made or purchased.

- Complete chair push-ups with hands flat on the chair or desk, try to lift the body up. This is wonderful for proprioceptive (deep pressure) input to the hands and arms. Make sure students are using their arms and not pushing up with their legs.
- Hook fingers together, one facing the ground and one facing the ceiling. Pull hands in opposite directions/against each other in resistance. This gives great proprioceptive input to both arms and even some core muscles.
- Squeeze balloons filled with sand, rice, or other neat textures to release muscle tension.
- Try to move pencils between thumb and each finger using only one hand. Also, rotate the pencil from the front to the back of the hand for an extra challenge. You could also use a ruler, erasers, or paper clips. Any item commonly found in the student's desk will work well.
- Make a "hand fidget box" with quiet items to play with such as paper clips, cotton balls, erasers, and fabric. Allow students time to play in the box. I've asked parents to send in items for the students/classroom and they are usually willing to help out!

My Students Can't Cut at Age Level During Center Time. How Do I Work on Cutting?

Using scissors is not only a necessary skill in school, it's vital to know how to cut as we progress through life. Imagine not having the ability to cut open a bag, package, or coupons! There is alot more to using scissors use than one might imagine. Make sure that the student's feet are firmly placed on the ground. Ensure that the student's position at the table is appropriate for his height. Practice rotating the paper in all directions with the "helper" hand. To hold the scissors, use a cue such as "thumbs up" consistently until the student can independently place hand into scissors correctly. Thumbs up is also the cue for ensuring that the thumb of the helper hand is on top of the paper to be cut. Place either the index plus middle fingers into the bottom loop or place only the middle finger in the bottom loop, leaving the index finger to help to support and guide the direction of the scissors. The remaining fingers should be tucked toward the palm. I have cut a small area out of the bottom of a sock to ensure that only the thumb, index, and middle fingers are exposed.

Teach the student to cut away from his body. Students tend to cut either toward or across their bodies. Bad habits form quickly, so monitor position closely in the beginning. Ensure that their shoulders are relaxed. The beginning of scissoring is not just learning to squeeze the scissors, but more importantly, learning to extend the fingers to release the scissors' hold on the paper. There are adapted scissors available if the student cannot release. They are either in a loop or include a small spring to release them once squeezed. It's always fun to use wording such as, "pretend the scissors are an alligator and make him chomp up the paper." Adding the use of fun ways to visualize can significantly increase a student's understanding of the task. Finally, make certain that the student's elbows are not "winging" or making "chicken wings." This means that elbows aren't sticking out from the sides of the body. Cue student to position elbows on the desk for extra stability.

- Right-Handed Students: Cut in an anti-clockwise direction.
- Left-Handed Students: Cut in a clockwise direction. Ensure that scissors designed for left-handed use are given to the student. One cannot succeed without the proper tools.

In What Order Do I Teach Cutting?

There is a typical developmental progression in cutting. When a student has difficulty cutting in the classroom, it is recommended that the student begins with the basics and moves through the steps in the order below. A student cannot cut complex shapes if he cannot cut on a straight line accurately.

- Students must learn how to open and close scissors. They can usually squeeze the scissors, but releasing may be difficult. Practice this part of cutting first. See the section above for information on how to teach the release.
- Begin cutting by making "fringe" or "feathers" (perfect for Thanksgiving) on a piece of paper. Paper plates can be used to cut around the edges and create a lion's mane. The lines should begin thick when beginning to cut. Most IEP goals for scissoring begin with students cutting a specified length on a thick line. The student progresses when he can cut further along thinner lines.
- Make cutting lines thicker with a black marker.
- Move on to cutting straight lines. There are many free pintables for cutting various lines on the internet. Cut strips of paper and staple or glue together to make chains. Strips can also be used to create paper pom-poms in school colors!
- Next, make the lines wavy and zigzagged. Gradually increase the difficulty and slope of the lines.
- Cutting squares, triangles, and polygons are less difficult than cutting out a circle. Circles require a constant movement of the paper by the "helper hand."
- Draw shapes almost the size of the paper, so that the student has to cut out only the corners or a small amount off of the edge to be successful.
- Complex shapes, such as stars, are the most difficult for students.
- Cut away the excess paper to make it easier to manipulate.
- The use of thinner card stock make squeezing the scissors more difficult, but makes the item to be cut stiffer and thus easier to hold with the "helper hand."

- Use coffee filters to make snowflakes and other fun patterns.
- OTs have plenty of fun ways to work on scissoring other than using paper!
- Cut straws and watch them fly across the table! String them later on for a cool necklace.
- Cut food items such as thin licorice, string cheese, cooked pasta of various shapes.
- Use putty to make a pretend "hot dog" and cut it into smaller pieces.
- Glitter glue, tape, or masking tape can be placed on the sides of the shape to be cut if a visual/tactile cue is needed.
- Cut items outside such as grass, weeds, or stems of thin plants. One year, we used our science experiment to practice cutting! We were working on seed germination and growth. We planted grass in small pots and watched it sprout and then grow. To trim the grass, we used our scissors! The kids enjoyed putting google eyes on the pots to pretend that the grass was hair.

Chapter 5

Autism Spectrum Disorders

Autism used to consist of specific categories: Asperger's syndrome; PDD-NOS, childhood disintegrative disorder, and autism. In 2004, I was told by my son's developmental pediatrician that he was "somewhere in the Asperger's category." That same year my younger son was diagnosed with PDD-NOS. As of the publication date of this book, and due to diagnostic changes, all children who had PDD-NOS, Asperger's syndrome, and autism are all now diagnosed with "autism." This can be quite difficult and confusing for parents. It's odd to think that all along your child has had Asperger's syndrome, for example, and now his diagnosis is autism. Since the new DSM V (5) was released in May of 2013, there have been huge changes in how autism is diagnosed. DSM stands for the Diagnostic and Statistical Manual. It's the universal book that clinicians use to make all mental health diagnoses. The book contains not only names of the disorders, but also criteria and descriptions. A vast number of clinicians use the manual and it is updated to reflect new research and updates as we learn more about cognitive (mental) disorders. According to the new DSM 5, "Individuals who have marked deficits in social communication, but whose symptoms do not otherwise meet criteria for autism spectrum disorder, should be evaluated for social (pragmatic) communication disorder."[5] As you can see, research is vast and is the driving force in how we learn about and understand ourselves.

There is no specific test which can determine autism, so clinicians look at many different checklists, parent and teacher interviews, observations, motor and adaptive skills assessments, and many other tests. Often times, many different clinicians contribute to the diagnostic procedure since autism affects many body systems. While it's important to note that as clinicians we should treat the individual, not the diagnosis, it's critical to obtain the most accurate diagnosis to receive appropriate services for your student. For example, Applied Behavior Analysis (ABA) is an excellent program for children with autism. In some states, there is a specific insurance approval/waiver to receive ABA, but you must have a diagnosis of autism to receive it.

What Is Autism?

The number of individuals with autism spectrum disorders is rising quickly. At the time of the publication of this book (May 2014), the Centers for Disease Control estimate that one in every sixty-eight children has autism![6] This is a staggering number and one that continues to rise quickly. Autism is four or five times more common in boys (one in every forty-two) than in girls (one in one hundred and eighty-nine). While there is no specific cause for autism, research is being done and certain genetic links, environmental factors, possible lack of oxygen during delivery, brain development concerns, and many other theories are emerging. There are even certain foods that many parents of children with autism avoid. They can include: preservatives, wheat, milk, dyes, chemicals, and more. Please remember to consult your physician prior to making any dietary changes.

Autism can cause decreases in social skills development, difficulty with motor skills, increases in repetitive behaviors, communication problems, restricted areas of interest, sensory processing problems, and more. For example, in early childhood, children often exhibit lack of eye contact with the caregiver/parent, decreased motor skills (fine and gross motor), decreased "turn-taking" in conversations (even in babbling for very young babies), difficulties or differences in sensory and motor processing (may fear loud noises, rub head along the floor, look at or move hands in front of eyes in unique ways, have difficulty tolerating various textures, avoid getting messy/dirty when playing). Many times parents begin therapy without knowing that the root cause of the child's issues is in fact autism. It's extremely important to participate in well baby/child check-ups as it's becoming more common to screen for autism and other developmental delays. The parent knows the child best and it's important to advocate for your child if you feel there's something not quite right.

What Can I Look for If I Suspect My Student Has Autism?

Autism spectrum disorders can affect every area of life. It's a huge misperception that students with autism do not have emotions. In fact, they have the same emotions as everyone else does. Speaking negatively about someone's weaknesses when they are present is not appropriate. It's best to either involve the student in the discussion when possible or ask that the conversation be moved to a different location. My own son appears not to be paying attention and engages in his computer program quite often, but he is listening and hears what we are saying! Always end discussions with a positive comment. Use interests and positive skills to help work on the ones which are weaker.

The following list contains areas in which some children with autism may have deficits. I tell every teacher I meet, "If you've met one child with autism, you've met one child with autism!" Autism is a spectrum diagnosis and there is a wide range of strengths and weaknesses a child with autism may show. Not every student with autism will exhibit weaknesses in coordination and some may excel at sports. Others will never gain the ability to speak verbally, while many will speak at a very early age. Remember, students are children first and their individual personality should be considered before their weaknesses are addressed. Use strengths and interests to work on weak areas. Your student will be more motivated and successes will follow!

- Students may have difficulty with fine motor skills which cause deficits in completing buttoning, snapping, tying, handwriting, scissoring, manipulating items at center time, and opening/closing lunch items and backpacks.
- Gross motor difficulties may include trouble hopping, skipping, participating in sports that require complex body movements, riding a bicycle, skating, performing core muscle movements, or using core muscles for stability.
- Self-care in areas of toileting, wiping nose/face, washing hands changing into and out of gym clothes, and other basic activities of daily living skills expected of students can be affected. Even getting jackets on and off can be a struggle.
- Socially, students may have difficulty making eye-contact, beginning and maintaining conversations, prefer to be alone, have trouble making/keeping friendships. This can be due to a number of factors such as: speech and language delays, unique body movements, difficulty with behaviors when stressed, or having areas of their own intense interest (may not consider that others do not have the same level of interest in the topic or not appropriate for student's age). Many children with autism do not have the ability to speak and use other ways to communicate such as computers, iPads, augmentative communication devices, sign language, pictures, etc.
- Difficulties processing sensory information. Often, the student's response does not match the intensity of the stimulus or the student does not

have the response we expect. For example, if bumped in the hallway the student may give a flight or fight (panic) response. Another example is when the fire alarm sounds, the student with autism may cover his ears and scream loudly or flee in panic.

- Transitions may be difficult. While we all crave routines, children with autism may have an extremely difficult time being flexible. Moving from task to task, place to place, or situation to the next situation may be hard for the student. He may require extra time, a visual chart or cue, or a countdown before transitions. Many students require an actual favorite toy or object when transitioning for extra security.

- Knowing or understanding abstract concepts such as time, money, and school subjects (e.g., reading comprehension) can be extremely difficult. Students with autism often need concrete examples.

- Difficulty processing auditory information. Most children with autism are visual learners. This means that they learn better with pictures and symbols which represent the concept they are learning. For example, we keep a visual schedule of our daily school schedule. It contains pictures and

Tell Me and I FORGET

Teach Me and I REMEMBER

Involve Me and I LEARN

words of the day's events and we adapt it for special events and for elective classes such as gym, foreign language study, art, music, etc. When we teach math, we use manipulatives which students can move, see, and touch. This dramatically helps their understanding of time, fractions, place value, and more. Also, it's important to build movement into our lessons. We jump and move when learning to spell words and math facts. It is amazing how many of us talk so much and so fast! It's important to slow down and take time to explain and demonstrate.

- Generalization of a task means that we learn how to complete an activity in one location and then are able to perform that same task in a different setting/environment. Students learn the basics of crossing the street at home and typically they can remember and perform the task of crossing the street at school or a friend's home. Children with autism can have great difficulty generalizing tasks. In essence, they know how to cross the street at home, yet cannot do it in a different setting. This can be extremely frustrating for them and for the person who is teaching them. It's not because they don't want to learn, but that it's difficult to transfer what they've learned to another place.

- Pre-occupation with a topic or interest. Students may be very well versed on their topic of intense interest but cannot tell you the steps of tying shoes or writing a position paper (even as a teenager). Often times, students are interested in one area that may or may not be age-appropriate. Usually, the student begins the "infatuation" or intense interest with their area when younger. Their knowledge is actually quite amazing and such areas may include, but certainly are not limited to: trains, letters, numbers, statistics, buses, cars, elevators, astronomy, fans, symbols, escalators, computers, manufacturing, maps, history, math facts, counting, etc. It's important to try and use the student's area of interest when teaching him. For example, exchange word problems about hockey for trains or astronomy.

- There can be a great discrepancy between a student's verbal level and his functional skill set. He may be able to perform several grade levels above his peers in one or more subjects, but be well below peers in another subject. It's extremely important to consider the student's cognitive or developmental levels vs. his age. The professionals who assess for autism and the treatment team should have various assessments/tests for areas of student strengths and weaknesses. It's also not uncommon for students with autism to have interests which are well above or way below his age. For example, the student may watch *Thomas the Train* cartoons as a pre-teen. Please allow for students to have this "down time" even if it seems silly to you. It is their way of relaxing and resting.

- Students may have different ways to move their bodies, eyes, hands, feet, etc. We call these "repetitive behaviors." They can look different in every student and may include rocking, moving hands in front of the eyes, flapping, walking in circles, repeating words or noises, spinning/twirling, moving their eyes or face, and lining up objects.

- Abstract and inferential thinking can be delayed or difficult to learn. Often times, reading comprehension can be extremely difficult. Asking and understanding the "W" questions (who, what, where, when, why) and how often require practice and can be hard to understand for students with autism. Identifying main ideas, identifying and explaining cause and effect, making predictions in a story, summarizing information, and even re-telling a story are areas in which students may struggle. It can be quite amazing though that many students with autism actually read early.

- Difficulties using speech appropriately can be quite common in students with autism. Remember that speech involves both expressive and receptive language. Both may be affected. Often times, students with autism may misuse pronouns. Many of my students mix up he, it, and she or use their name vs saying "I." Additionally, students may use "scripting" or memorizing scripts (such as in a play or dialogue). There have been many students I've worked with who can repeat entire episodes of their favorite movie, television show, or cartoon. It's truly amazing, but in place of conversation they may insert a specific like that's related in some way to the topic. Here's an example: I was happy that one of my students printed the letter "d" properly. I said, "Great work, David!" and he replied, "He shoots and he scores, this has been an amazing win for the Penguins." Obviously, he had the right idea with the fact that it was a happy event, but the script from the hockey game was something he'd memorized. It didn't quite fit the situation. We then practiced some exchanges which would be more socially appropriate.

- Skills involving social language (pragmatics) may be significantly impaired. Our society is filled with complicated social rules, hard to understand language (idioms, homophones, sarcasm, irony, double meanings), and vocal tones signifying different emotions. Even without any communication problems, it can be difficult to navigate our language! For example, when someone asks, "How are you today?" they often do not want an answer, but are simply being friendly. Knowing when to stop talking and switch topics, reading someone's body language are often make-or- break skills in conversation. Remember that students with autism often have areas of pre-occupation because they may have difficulty knowing when to stop talking about these areas and have such a vast knowledge base about them, that they can go on and on for extended periods of time. Other students may be quickly bored or not have those same interests and often walk away from the conversation. Reciprocation and turn- taking are required for a conversation between two people. It's critical to "read" the conversation partner's signals in order to continue conversing. Students with autism can have a great deal of trouble interpreting pragmatics. Telling and interpreting jokes and sarcasm can be extremely difficult. We even encourage students to learn jokes and "rehearse" humor and laughing after a joke is told. My son's therapist used to teach him from a joke book. He's since learned to tell a few jokes that make his peers chuckle!

- Another difficulty with social interaction is understanding body language and position. It's important not to stand too closely to the person you're speaking with. Personal space is another area in which students with autism may have difficulty. We use hula hoops or simply stretch out our arms. This is the appropriate amount of space required to keep a comfortable distance. Speech and language therapy, help from teachers or guidance counselors to facilitate peer interactions, and small groups can help and should be included in the education plan. For example, holding a "lunch buddy program" with peers who had similar interests was an extremely successful program in many schools I've worked in. An aide or counselor helped to facilitate language and keep conversations moving and on-topic. Remember that effective communication with other students can build self-confidence. Skills build upon each other as students practice them in isolation and then in peer groups. Humans need to have successful social interactions to get needs met and gain skills for future jobs, interviews, and life itself. When we notice that a particular student is struggling with peer interaction, it's our job to assist them in any way possible. It's critical to remember that school is where we learn academic and social skills that we will use for a lifetime.

- Behavior and impulse control can be areas of weakness for students with autism. This is an area that is difficult for many children. Considering the developmental age of the student vs. the chronological age, is important when making the educational plan. Please remember that autism does not cause bad behavior. Just because a student has autism does not mean that he will behave badly. As with any student, lack of understanding, sensory processing difficulties, frustration, social skills deficits, communication issues, lack of impulse control, difficulty with rationalization, and many other issues can contribute to behavioral outbursts. Behavior is communication and we should be detectives to determine the root cause. See Chapter 7 for strategies to help with behavior.

- Books such as Jennifer O'Toole's *Asperkids*™ are supportive and encouraging to children, teens, and adults with autism.

What Is a Co-Morbid Condition?

Often times, students who have been diagnosed with autism or any other cognitive and medical need can have another disability or diagnosis which affects them. We call this a co-morbid condition. It's not at all uncommon for our students to have one or more of these conditions. For example, when a student is diagnosed with autism it does not automatically mean that he has a sensory processing disorder. They are two separate diagnoses that often (but not always) come together. Often times, students with autism can have ADHD, dysgraphia, another learning disorder, gastro-intestinal issues, allergies, and many more. In fact, any child with special needs can have one or more co-morbid conditions. This is why it's our responsibility to pour through the student's specific information and make decisions based on that student only. We should never fit any two students into one box as their individual needs, medical history, and personality all affect their learning.

What Are Some Specific Things That Should Be Included in the Educational Plan for Students Who Have Autism?

Since autism spectrum disorders can affect many areas of education, there should be many adaptations and modifications tailored toward each student.

Considering transition skills, behavior, fine and gross motor, sensory processing deficits, social skills, learning disorders, and any unique need of the student is important to formulating the best educational plan possible. Behavior plans should be implemented when needed. Note any sensory responses (both hypo and hyper-responsiveness) along with any flight or fight responses that cause adverse physical reactions. Providing an outlet or safe place for students with these responses needs to be planned for prior to the actual event, so everyone on the team is prepared. Students should feel safe at school, because so much of their time is spent there. Of course, the optimal learning environment should be comfortable and safe for every student in the classroom.

The creation of visuals, social stories, and schedules is critical to support many students with autism. It's important to remember that all students learn in different ways. Some learn by hearing the information and repeating it. They use their auditory system to learn new concepts and review old ones. Others learn by movement and are called kinesthetic learners. Building movement activities and using manipulatives in the classroom or during homework will help these students to remember facts, spelling words, and other abstract information. Students who learn visually benefit from schedules posted in the classroom, by having visual representations of concepts such as time and money. Social Stories™ are an example of a visual review of a specific situation and the appropriate reaction the student should have to it. For example, fire drills are unexpected and can be extremely difficult for any student. If the student is very fearful of unexpected noises, a file alarm can cause a true panic reaction. I've had many students truly panic and flee the situation. This can cause a dangerous situation for the student. A social story is a way for us to create a student-specific story to fit the unique situation. It's best to use the student's name, his strengths, pictures of the environment and the actual setting, along with what the desired behavior and safe way to deal with the situation should be. Provide examples of ways the student should act when the fire alarm sounds. "When I hear a fire alarm, I can put on my noise-cancelling headphones." "When I feel confused I will not yell, I will raise my hand and wait for my teacher to call on me." "Sometimes, I have too much anger. When I feel this way, I can choose an activity from the menu and ask to move to the take-a- break room." These are some examples of ideas for stories. Make sure to read and review them often so that the student is familiar with the actions he is supposed to take when he's working through his feelings or anxiety. Knowing the plan is extremely helpful when unexpected speed bumps occur.

For information on specific areas of weakness in children who have autism, please refer to the specific chapter. For example, please see Chapter 6 on Sensory Processing Disorders for specific concerns about a student's visual response and the modifications recommended to help him in that area. If he's having issues with attention, see chapter 8 on ADHD and organization. Every accommodation listed is appropriate for students having difficulties in the area—no matter what the diagnosis or reason behind the problem is.

What Can I Do for Teens/Young Adults as They Transition out of School?

Education law requires team discussion about transition planning. It is the responsibility of the team to formulate a plan that fits the student's abilities, addresses social skills, behaviors, and independent living skills. It's never too early to begin planning. The student's teachers have great knowledge about his performance with skills that he will need in order to secure gainful employment. This makes both special and general education teachers integral members of the planning team.

Community integration and participation in vocational planning is critical for life-long success. It is important to involve students in planning whenever possible. I always encourage students to participate in the IEP/goal-setting process when appropriate. Empowering students by giving them choices and options can significantly increase participation and self-esteem. Integration of the student's strengths and interests can benefit him and assist in the best vocational choices. Goal setting for social skills training, vocational skill training, and community integration opportunities should occur and then be implemented in the student's least restrictive environment. Meetings with counselors to discuss college options and possible majors, vocational options, and special community programming (e.g., as sheltered workshops) should happen regularly. Data should be collected regularly and programs/instructions adapted when needed. Activities for students to practice their social and life skills should be incorporated so that students have ample opportunity to rehearse in a variety of settings. This is best for generalization of skills into real-life situations.

Chapter 5 Resources

www.asperkids.com	Asperkids
www.autism.com	Autism Research Institute
www.autismnow.org	Autism NOW
www.autism-society.org	Autism Society of America
www.autismspeaks.org	Autism Speaks
www.cdc.gov	Centers for Disease Control and Prevention
www.nationalautism association.org	National Autism Association
www.ninds.nih.gov	National Institute for Neurological Disorders and Stroke
www.researchautism.org	Organization for Autism Research
www.spdfoundation.net	Sensory Processing Disorder Foundation
www.tacanow.org	TACA (Talk About Curing Autism)

Chapter 6

Sensory Processing Disorder in School

Overview of Sensory Processing Disorder:

Sensory processing disorder (SPD) was called Sensory Integration (SI) dysfunction in past years. The name has changed as researchers have learned more about sensory processing. "Dr. A. Jean Ayres, a researcher and pioneer of this field, coined the term Sensory Integration Dysfunction. She used the term throughout her professional career (1954-1988) to describe atypical social, emotional, motor, and functional patterns of behavior that were related to poor processing of sensory stimuli." (SPDFoundation.net)[7]

What Does Sensory Processing Mean?

Our success in our daily functioning is dependent directly on the input or information we receive through our senses, our processing of that input, and our formulation of the correct output or response. If you'll remember from the first book, *The Pocket Occupational Therapist*, Chapter 5, there are more than the five senses we traditionally think of. Proprioception and vestibular senses are critical as they help our bodies to determine position in space, movement, and light vs. heavy touch. Our body's perception, processing, and response all happen at a sub-conscious level. There are many ways information enters and is perceived by our bodies and then based on how we take in that information and process it (based on our unique experiences); we formulate an output or response. Everyone perceives sensory information differently because we have all had different life experiences.

The following is a chart based on the proposed nosology by SPD expert Dr. Lucy Jane Miller.

Sensory Processing Disorder	
Sensory-Based Motor Disorder (SBMD)	Sensory Over-Responsivity (SOR) Sensory Under-Responsivity (SUR) Sensory Craving (SC)
Sensory Modulation Disorder (SMD)	Dyspraxia Postural Disorder
Sensory Discrimination Disorder (SDD)	Visual Auditory Tactile Taste/Smell Position/Movement Interoception

*Miller LJ, Anzalone ME, Lane SJ, Cermak SA, Osten ET. (2007) Concept evolution in sensory integration: A proposed nosology for diagnosis. *American Journal of Occupational Therapy. 61* (2), 135-140.[8]

Modulation is the balance between our level of arousal and the intensity of the stimulation we are experiencing. Our body's modulation helps determine our response to the environment. The problem comes when someone has sensory processing dysfunction. The level of response may not fit the level required or may not fit the situation.

Refer to the chart at the top of this page. You will notice that Sensory-Based Motor Disorder has three sub-types. Sensory Over- Responsivity (SOR); Sensory Under-Responsivity (SUR); and Sensory Craving (SC). Some people have heightened arousal levels (hypersensitive), low arousal levels (hyposensitive), are cravers or have mixed levels. The most important point is that the reactions our bodies have to the information we receive can affect our heart rate, temperature, sweating, blood vessels, digestion, etc. How would you react if a lizard began crawling up your leg? Some would "freak out" and scream, sweat, or cry. Others may simply reach down and remove the animal without much thought. So, if you had a pet lizard as a child, you may not respond in the same way as someone who is extremely afraid of reptiles.

Everyone exists at a different level of sensory alertness. For a successful existence, a person needs to be able to receive and process sensory input. Consider a fire drill. To the school principal, it is an important safety drill. He may be excited to see how the hard work in training his staff will pay off. A fireman observing may feel a sense of pride and remember all of the successes he's had in over 20 years of fighting fires. The classroom teacher may feel that the drill is a disruption in teaching. One of the students in the classroom may feel happy and view the drill as a great way to escape instruction time and to get some fresh air outside. Another student may perceive the fire drill as a noise that is terrifying and makes her body feel horribly. She may actually be moved into a "flight or fight" response where her heart rate increases, her stress hormone (cortisol) is released, and she may flee the situation and demonstrate inappropriate behavior along the way. The same situation feels totally different to everyone in that school due to each person's prior experience and their current state of alertness.

What do we take away from the above scenario? Our existence in the situation we are in right now depends on our experiences prior to this point in time. This is true for every person and our children with sensory processing disorder are no exception. A student may wake up after a restless night of sleep. He may be agitated and hyperresponsive to noise, the feeling of his clothing as he gets dressed, the feeling of the crunchy, pinchy cereal he's eating for breakfast, the noise of the school bus as the children talk on the way to school. He is already operating at a heightened level of alertness and he is hyperresponsive.

We expect him to sit in his seat quietly and pay attention to hours of classroom instruction. He may exhibit disruptive behaviors as a result of his attempts to organize himself and then have his recess taken away as a punishment. He may have a tantrum not due to "bad" or attention-seeking behavior, but due to his frustration. It is our jobs as parents, teachers, and therapists to play detective and to help our children figure out their general baseline and triggers to sensory overload. We should make lists, charts, and do whatever is necessary to help learn about our children's sensory systems.

Here are some things to look for in your classroom for each type of sensory-responsiveness. The sensory cravers, simply seek sensory input and will do what it takes to seek it. They may constantly crash into others, make noises with their mouths during class time, appear disruptive, and have difficulty sitting still.

Out of the Pocket Activity

What to Look for When Considering Hypersensitivity (SOR) Sensory Over-Responsivity:

- Sensory input seems to be too much or too often.

- Fear of loud noises or overreaction to un-expected noises throughout the school day.
- Hypersensitive to smells or tastes. Packs same food for lunch every day with little variation.
- Over-reaction to touch from other children or when accidentally bumped in class or when in line.
- Agitation when standing close to others in line or sitting in a crowded setting such as a cafeteria, assembly, and public place.
- Meltdowns during center time due to textures, getting messy, painting, and glue projects.
- Difficulty transitioning between summer and winter clothing. May wear inappropriate clothing for season.
- Agitation during restroom breaks or when washing hands.
- Reluctance to go to art, music, or gym due to noise, smell, or non-structure.
- Poor visual integration (seems lost in space).

What to Look for When Considering Hyposensitivity (SUR – Sensory Under-Responsivity)

- This student has difficulty taking cues or information from his environment.
- Crave movement activities, twirling, spinning, swinging, and jumping constantly during the day.
- Difficulty sitting still in chair. May fidget with hands and pick at nails or body.
- Presses too hard on paper when writing.
- Holds pencil with "immature grasp" or too many fingers on the utensil.
- Impulsivity and dangerous behaviors such as jumping off of high playground equipment without considering the consequences.

- Difficulty with processing directions and sounds.
- Delays in speech with pronunciation and focusing on foreground sounds.
- May have difficulty with awareness of personal space or have trouble "keeping hands to self."
- Poor coordination during visual tasks.
- Enjoys making sounds. Often makes constant noise with mouth or tapping tools on desk. May be distraction to classroom.
- Reacts inappropriately to others' feelings.
- May not notice injury.
- Smells objects or people in the classroom.
- Mouths objects frequently that aren't food or aren't age-appropriate. Includes chewing on pencils, glue, clothing (sleeves or neck), or drools often.
- May have toileting difficulty or frequent "accidents."

Mixed Hypo-Hyper Frequently Occurs and Any of the Above Can Occur Along with the Following:

- Writes too hard/soft with pencil.
- Reacts with anger, sadness, fear to social situations.
- May avoid interaction in social situations.
- May not consider others' feelings.
- Difficult to calm down once upset.
- Has difficulty with transitioning and completing tasks.

Here's an example:

Joshua has hypersensitivity or SOR. He quickly becomes over- excited and is distracted by every stimulus around him. He is still wearing shorts and a t-shirt even though it's December and snowing outside. Today, he is sitting in the classroom for his math class. He cannot screen out sounds, sights, smells, and tactile/touch items which are not appropriate to the teacher's lecture. It is virtually impossible to attend to the teacher's voice and SMART® Board. What does she experience? The classroom temperature may be too hot; he hears the buzzing of the fluorescent lights; he is annoyed by the sound of his pencil sliding across the paper; the chair he's sitting on is too hard; someone just sneezed and he's worried about the spread of germs; he smells lunch baking in the cafeteria. The list may go on and on. He truly wants to focus on the math lesson, but he becomes irritated and agitated. He has nowhere to place his irritated energy. His body may feel anxiety when his heartbeat increases, he begins to sweat, and he may even begin to breathe rapidly. Joshua quickly becomes tearful and begins to scream. When he receives discipline, he throws his book on the floor and loses recess. The irony of the situation, though, is that Joshua would truly benefit from attending recess to get necessary activities to help him to regulate his body. This is a common situation and unfortunately, it can be a vicious cycle for kids with difficulty integrating their sensory systems.

What Is a Sensory Craver (SC)?

Sensory craving means that it is an intense desire (craving) to seek out sensory input. The difference between a sensory craver and sensory- under responsive student is that children who are cravers can become even more disorganized as they seek more and more input. Sensory cravers benefit from breaking down sensory activities and inserting functional tasks. For example, a child who is a craver cannot get enough of smelling things. She smells every object she can and keeps this up with no end in sight. OTs who are specifically trained in SPD and its treatment know how to help and how to correctly apply sensory techniques.

I am often asked by parents and new therapists why I don't let a child spin and spin at his will on my clinic's suspension equipment. It's critical to understand the correct application of sensory input. Swinging can actually be disorganizing to a child's sensory system. The child needs to be limited or he risks side-effects of too much spinning (rotary input). Some of these include: nausea, headache, and decreased alertness. This happened to my own son when his therapist was untrained in SPD and permitted him to spin and spin. Spinning should be limited to a few rotations and then by adding a functional task such as crawling on all fours to pick up a piece of a puzzle. I recommend that caregivers add lots of activities which give the student "heavy work" or proprioceptive input. See "Adding Calming Strategies" on page 102 for more details and ideas for this type of input.

Are There Any Other Signs and Symptoms of SPD?

Students may have difficulties in many areas if they have difficulty processing the information they receive from their environment. Here are a few additional considerations:

- Visual-perceptual deficits should be considered. If the classroom is too "busy" or colorful, it may actually be overwhelming for the child with SPD.
- Difficulty with knowing right from left and moving either arm across the middle of their body. (See Chapter 3, page 35.)
- Difficulty going up and down steps, climbing on the playground, or walking up/down the bleachers.
- Trouble with finger plays or games such as "Simon Says" or the "Hokey Pokey."
- Walks on his toes often. This should be evaluated by a physician as tight heel cords may result from walking on toes for a prolonged period. My own son required casts on both of his feet due to his "toe-walking" from sensory processing disorder. To help, come up with a cue such as "heels" or hold up a picture of a foot to remind students.
- Toileting skills delayed due to decreased awareness of the student's body/ sensory under-responsivity.

- Low self-esteem or high anxiety. Children who are not consistently successful at tasks they attempt to complete everyday tend to become anxious or depressed. Remember, SPD affects more than we—teachers, caregivers, or therapists—may realize, and the student's emotions should be considered in treatment planning.

*What Is Interoception?**

We are all individuals because of what we look like, what our beliefs are, and how we feel on the inside. Every individual experiences the world around him uniquely. Interoception is the way our body feels pain, interprets senses, experiences hunger and thirst, and helps us with our heart rhythms, sleep cycles, and bowel movements. The nerve endings placed throughout our internal organs are responsible for how we "feel" things internally. So, students who have had difficulty with toilet training may not actually feel the sensation of having to "go." People with difficulty feeling hunger may not eat even though their bodies need nutrition at the time. This can result in difficulty knowing when it's time to use the potty and frequent accidents or constipation. Additionally, hunger and thirst can be affected. If your child with SPD is under weight or not eating properly, she may not be recognizing the "cues" her body is giving her that she's actually hungry.

*What Is Dyspraxia?***

Children with dyspraxia have difficulties with motor learning. It's a sensory-based motor disorder. Praxis means the ability to plan and then execute

---

* Tsakiris M, Tajadura-Jimenez A & Costantini M (2011). Just a heartbeat away from one's body: interoceptive sensitivity predicts malleability of body representations. Proceedings of the Royal Society, B, *Biological Sciences. 278* (1717):2470-6. [9]

** Fisher, Murray & Bundy, *Sensory Integration: Theory and Practice*, 1991, F.A. Davis Company, p. 141.[10]

movement, and adding DYS means difficulty with. The areas of difficulty include planning (ideation), making the plan in the correct order (sequencing), and carrying out that plan. An OT might look at the following activity:

Brushing Teeth

- Thinking about the activity. "I need to brush my teeth."
- Going to the sink where the activity takes place.
- Picking up the toothbrush.
- Picking up the toothpaste.
- Opening up the toothpaste.
- Squeezing the toothpaste on to the brush.
- Putting the lid back on the toothpaste tube.
- Bringing the toothbrush to the mouth.
- Brushing each area carefully.
- Spitting out the residual paste.
- Rinsing mouth out, which involves its own set of motor skills

As you can see there are many different steps at which a person with dyspraxia may have difficulty. It's especially challenging for a person with dyspraxia to learn new concepts.

Dyspraxia causes many difficulties starting, planning, and completing activities. It can affect people throughout their lives and in many different areas. Because we form motor plans for every move we make, it can be extremely frustrating to have dyspraxia. Dyspraxia may be evident in many areas including: speech, taking care of daily activities, eating, sleeping, banking, shopping, writing, organizing, sports, concentrating, cutting, and many more. Children with dyspraxia may have difficulty tolerating unexpected touch or loud noises. Often, students with dyspraxia may have difficulties with knowing where their bodies are in space and can become disoriented when up-side down. This is why it's important to consider accommodations that a child with dyspraxia needs in order to be successful at school. As you move through the list of accommodations in each area, consider which would be helpful to your student with dyspraxia.

Students with dyspraxia need encouragement to succeed and often benefit from a visual outline of the steps to take for an activity. They can have success with positive reinforcement, sensory integration training (with a qualified OT), visual and verbal cues such as picture schedules that break tasks down according to their individual steps; and using words such as: "What's the next step," or "What comes next?"

Visit www.dyspraxiausa.org for additional information, signs, and common symptoms by age.

What Is Postural Disorder? ***

Students who have postural disorder often have difficulty picking up sensory cues. They may exhibit some of the signs listed under the previous sub-section on Sensory Hyposensitivity or Sensory Under- Responsiveness. They may have difficulty with maintaining their posture and slouch often. Children with postural disorder are often seen in a "W" sitting position (see left photo). They have difficulty maintaining their stable base of support. As a result, their posture and subsequently their coordination in arms and legs may be affected. Remember, the body's core is the base of the pyramid.

What does a child with postural disorder "look like?" They may have difficulty with activities requiring their entire body to move in a coordinated way. Students may have difficulty:

***   Miller, L.J., Collins, B. (2012) Sensory Solutions: Sensory –Based Motor Disorders: Postural Disorder
       Autism Asperger's Digest [11]

- navigating the playground equipment;
- participating in gym class due to difficulty with jumping jacks, skipping, scooters, sit-ups, and games;
- experience low self-esteem due to their desire to participate and match other students without SPD coupled with the frustration of not being able to succeed no matter how hard they try;
- with increased fatigue and slouching at their desk when writing assignments;
- completing prolonged physical activity (compared with typically developing peers) or physical demands;
- startle or fight-or-flight responses to movement against gravity (such as swinging, crawling, touching toes) or when movement is unexpected;
- may lean against another student, shelving, or wall during circle time.

What Accommodations Are Recommended for Students with Sensory Processing Disorder?

Since each student's sensory system is different and his/her response to input is varied, I've broken down accommodations into the area of concern. Many of the ideas listed can be used in different settings and can be combined with activities in other areas. For example, if your student is fidgeting with his hands and feet plus is frequently chewing on his shirt, you may choose activities from a few areas.

Remember that pushing, pulling, lifting, chores, and carrying activities are generally calming and provide the proprioceptive (heavy work) input to students. A child should not be spun in a rotary manner in any swing in the sensory room without an OT trained in sensory processing techniques. Spinning in this way can cause serious implications and affects can last from six to eight hours. In general, discourage a child from spinning as it can be disorganizing. Instead, offer a trampoline or jumping activity. Other options can include swinging on the playground, bouncing on a ball, sliding, using a BOSU® ball, a scooter, etc. These activities are still stimulating the vestibular system, but in a much more organizing way. In my first book, *The Pocket Occupational Therapist for Families of Children with Autism and Special Needs*, I provided many activity ideas such as lying on your belly while doing puzzles, games, etc.

When a child moves around on a daily basis, rolls upside-down (inverted against gravity), runs, or changes position there is an impact on his vestibular system. This system is so important as it registers movement while we go through planes (vertical, horizontal, and diagonal). Vestibular movement is extremely important to a young baby's development and the need continues throughout our lifetime to calm and regulate. When we have a head cold and feel dizzy with movement, our vestibular system is impacted and the results are noticeable. The vestibular system is quite complicated and involves many parts of the body, including the ears and brain. For a full explanation of the vestibular system, ask your individual OT and check out the following resources:

- Sensory Processing Disorder Foundation with Dr. Lucy Jane Miller (www.spdfoundation.net)
- A Sensory Life by Angie Voss, OTR (www.asensorylife.com)
- *Raising a Sensory Smart Child* by Lindsey Biel OTR/L and Nancy Peske (www.sensorysmarts.com)

OUT OF THE POCKET ACTIVITY

Fidgeting with Hands and Feet

- Use fidget toys such as the Koosh ball, Tangle Jr., Fuzzy Tangle or make your own out of fleece, burlap, balloons (often filled with sand or rice),

The Special Needs SCHOOL Survival Guide

and Lycra to place under the desk or in the student's pocket. There are many types of "fidget toys" available in catalogues for children with special needs or on Amazon.

- Place Velcro on the bottom of the student's desk, so he may run fingers along its texture. Add Velcro hook side (rough side) to the desk bottom and the loop side (smooth side) to a wooden ball or spool. The student has to move the items around underneath his desk from one side to the other without looking. Other fabrics such as burlap, velvet, felt, and cotton may be used. Experiment with fabrics and textures to see what works best for your student.

- Pumice, sand paper, and other abrasive textures make wonderful (and inexpensive) fidgets.

- Place smooth stones in the pocket or in a fabric pouch.

- Wrap exercise band around legs of chair or two legs of the desk so that the student may gain input to his legs.

- Use "standing desks" with higher stools so that students who are unable to sit for long periods of time, may stand up. Try the "Standing Desk Conversion Kit" (www.flaghouse.com).

- Use foot fidgets, such as Foot-Shaped steppers (www.therapyshoppe. com), Foot Fidget Footrest (www.funandfunction.com).

- Bean bags, "HowdaHUGS®" seats (www.howda.com), T-stools, rocking chairs, and ball chairs are all ideas for seating in a classroom.

- BOSU® balls are excellent for use in yoga, exercise, and for seating. They provide a great core muscle workout—awesome for proprioceptive input or heavy work.

Chewing on Shirts, Pencils, or Other Items and Making Noise with Mouth

It's important to remember that chewing may be incredibly calming to some students. Often, when people are feeling stressed or overwhelmed, they either eat or place something into their mouths. Chewing items such as pencils, gum, ice chips, candy, and biting nails are all "acceptable" grown-up behaviors.

- Use items such as Chewlery® or Sentio- CHEWS® (see photo to the right, courtesy of www.kidcompanions) that are wearable and safe for placing into the mouth. There are some cool designs for both boys and girls which look like regular necklaces students might wear.

- Latex-free clear aquarium tubing can easily be placed on the top of the writing utensil. I recommend a three inch piece.
- Allow gum chewing in class. Mint flavor is generally alerting.
- Hard candy with hollow centers, pretzels, and crackers may be eaten during class time.
- Permit students to use a sports bottle with spout to sip on water throughout the day. This may increase concentration for all students.
- Blow bubbles at recess.
- Chewigem (www.chewigem.com) offers colorful bangles and pendants for students. Designs are fun and colorful!
- Drink through smaller, thinner straws at lunch. Drink box straws make the mouth muscles work harder than a straw that's wider.
- Looped straws require extra work from the oral muscles.
- Purchase ARK's Grabbers (see photo courtesy of www.ARKTherapeutic.com). They provide excellent oral input!

- Use of specialized cushions for seating (see next section) can help with students who hum or make noises with their mouths.
- Sew together pieces of Lycra or fleece to make a "necklace" that's longer than the student's collar and that he can pull to his mouth to "chew" on. This is better and can be switched out during the day if too much saliva is present, but it is not for smaller children and must be monitored due to strangulation/choking hazard.
- Purchase sports type wrist bands so that students can chew or fidget with them when necessary. They also are great saliva absorbers!
- Pencil toppers can come in many fun colors, shapes, and sizes, which are affordable. Visit Amazon.com or any special needs catalogue.

Adding Calming Strategies

Many students with SPD benefit from heavy work activities. It is generally accepted that the addition of activities which provide increased input to muscles in the areas of push, pull, lift, and carry are calming. There are many appropriate activities that can be added to the classroom for students who may fidget, have difficulty sitting still, need to stand up often, and have difficulty knowing where their bodies are in space. Heavy work affects the reticular formation in the brainstem, which has control on muscle reflexes and muscle tone. Signals are sent to this area which interprets the sensory and movement signals from the various parts of the student's body.

- Use of weighted lap pad of beans, sand, or rice. Vibratory pillows such as those created by Senseez (www.senseez.com) are great since they provide calming input as students sit on them.
- Wrap up in Lycra fabric or body socks.
- Use the manual pencil sharpener.

- Use vibrating pens. These can often be found at local discount stores. When I see them, I buy several since they tend to be tossed around or can roll off of student's desks.
- Use vibratory toys such as the vibrating snake at www.achievement-products.com.
- Use desk carrels. They are available in wood or cardboard and can be found at many school sites including www.SchoolOutfitters.com.
- Ask students to carry books to another classroom or the library.
- Crawl on all fours like a crab, dog, etc. to transition between classes or in the classroom for breaks (if age appropriate).
- Play Twister®, and the Hokey Pokey.
- "Spot Markers" (see picture right) can be purchased from www.FunandFunction.com. Students can work on body part.

- identification, left/right, and heavy work such as crawling to red dot, tip-toe to blue dot, etc. Spot markers are also awesome visual cues for where to sit or stand for circle time, line leaders, while waiting for their turn, and more.
- Spot Markers Photo Courtesy of www.FunandFunction.com.
- Make an "activity of the day" that students perform while transitioning. Ideas can include hopping, skipping, limbo, and jumping over a taped line.
- Use a weighted backpack during transition times or between classes. Most middle and high school students do this as they transfer from building to building. Adding a few books if the backpack is too light may help.
- Use the gym or exercise room and move mats and other heavier equipment.
- Crawl through Lycra tunnels from place to place.
- Try ankle or arm weights (not too heavy).

- Use a cushion filled with air or gel (like the one pictured on the previous page courtesy of FunandFunction.com) on the chair so student's core/postural muscles must work harder to support his body. They are available in a rainbow of colors! Some are even textured for extra input.

- Wall-pushups can be done with the entire classroom prior to a long lecture or assignment.

- Placing hands on the arms or seat of the chair and then pushing bum up to a count of 10 is great heavy work while seated. Be sure not to use the legs to help!

- Stapling papers onto the cork board or bulletin board is great heavy work.

- Tape worksheets to the walls so that students have to stand up and move around to do their work. This movement break is a nice change from sitting at the desk.

- Use weighted blankets, lap pads, stuffed animals, clothing (such as hats and suspenders), or weighted vests. The vest is worn for a specified period of time and its weight is no more than 5% of the student's body weight. At no time should the child's head be covered under a weighted blanket.

- Compression vests are an extremely beneficial intervention. They are worn by students underneath their clothing. Stabilizing Pressure Input Orthosis (SPIO™) garments are designed with Lycra to provide even compression throughout the area they cover. Unlike weighted vests, there is no time limit for their use (www.spioworks.com).

- Many large and private companies maketighter/stretchable fabric clothing in all colors. Try local sporting goods stores for bargains first!

- CDs such as *Sound-Eaze* and *School-Eaze* (www.pocketot.com) can help to prepare students for noises that are found in the community and at school. The CDs are designed not for headphones, but for open air use. The noises include sirens, fire drill, and cafeteria. Each track is set to basic rhythms so that the student feels the steady beat.

- Erase and wash chalk and white boards.
- Move chairs to the top of the desks at the end of the day or ask students to empty trash or recycle bin as "classroom helper."
- BOSU® balls are excellent for use in yoga, exercise, and for seating. They provide a great core muscle workout—awesome for proprioceptive input or heavy work.

Circle or Group Time

- Tape areas off into blocks on the carpet or circle time area. Providing a visual space may help students to realize personal space.
- Use the visual of a hula hoop or the verbalization "Stretch your arms straight out from your sides. This is how much space should be between you and your friends" to identify personal space.
- Make an X on the area where the child should place his bottom.
- Allow student with SPD to assist you in handing out supplies.
- Use a T-stool. It's a stool made out of wood and shaped like the upper case letter T. Its purpose is to allow students to use their core muscles to balance. It's a great way to provide heavy work to the body's core muscles. See photo for an example of a T-Stool with rocker base (www.FunandFunction.com).
- Allow students to sit on bean bags. This may increase the attention of the entire classroom!
- Use a curtain to block off visually complex areas such as bookshelves so students aren't distracted.
- Allow students to lay on their tummies while listening to a story or while thinking creatively.

- Use weighted lap pads or fidget items to increase attention.
- Hokki stools are unique and can be purchased on the Internet. They come in four sizes and five different colors. The stools allow for movement in all directions while a person is seated. It's fabulous for working core muscles and for providing sensory input. Here is a website for more information: www.vs.de/en/hokki.

Movement-Based Activities in Any Class

- Ask students to jump/hop right if the answer is true and hop to the left if the answer is false.
- Use rhythms to repeat spelling word lists.
- Create your own buzzer, use a bell, or purchase "Answer Buzzers" (www.exceptionalteaching.net) for a fun way to answer classroom questions.
- Make teams and toss beach balls back and forth while listing or answering multiplication facts and vocabulary words.
- Tape the letter of the day on the floor and ask students to stop and stand on it while moving from place to place. When the student is standing on the letter, name three words that begin with that letter. Try it with Math facts too!
- Use S'Cool Moves (www.schoolmoves.com) as a classroom- based movement program.
- Wave scarves or light fabric, such as chiffon, to a rhythm or music.
- Drive Through Menus were created by an OT and are simple and easy exercises when time is limited. They are great for mini-breaks before focus is needed (www.allthepossibilitiesinc.com).
- Musicians Greg and Steve (www.gregandsteve.com) offer a variety of awesome movement CDs. I have used them in my clinic and school settings with wonderful success.

- The Vital Links program offers unmodified (not part of their official Therapeutic Listening ® program) CDs for use in open air, or without headphones. They are great, upbeat, and can be used along with their activity booklet (www.vitallinks.net). Ask your OT for more details.
- Play balloon volleyball or see how long each student can keep a balloon up in the air. This is a quiet task that can be completed with some nice success since the balloon is light and slow moving.

Visual Supports

Students may have difficulty seeing words on paper, copying from the board, and become overwhelmed with too much visual input. It is often so exciting for teachers to set up their classrooms for the year. Websites such as Pinterest® and Teachers Pay Teachers® are allowing for a great deal of activity and idea sharing. It's critical to remember that reducing clutter is very important to those who are easily distracted. Using bright colors and big posters looks beautiful to some and is torture to others!

OUT OF THE POCKET ACTIVITY

- Copy worksheets onto pastel colored paper. Generally blue and green are calming and red and orange are alerting.
- Enlarge print and use simple fonts.
- It's easy to get creative and use fancy fonts, but they can be difficult to read.
- Minimize classroom decorations and colors. Additionally, minimize distractions near the teaching area or blackboard.
- Use touch-screen technology vs. keyboard and mouse.
- Seat the student near the board or teaching area, so he's not distracted by

watching other students or movement in the classroom.

- Ask students to repeat directions verbally to ensure understanding.
- Break directions down into more manageable steps.
- Purchase filters for fluorescent lighting. They can be bought in several colors. Some are made of fabric and some (more expensive) are created to look like ocean scenes. Many dentists' offices are using them above the chairs when clients get fillings.
- Use colored overlays or filters when reading. Visit the following website for more information: www.Irlen.com.
- Use a contrasting color when writing important dates, such as tests and due dates.
- Place a model or finished example on the students desk.
- Provide the opportunity to observe another student performing a task first as an example.
- To prevent the student from looking up from his paper to the board and back again multiple times; provide a copy of what is written on the chalkboard. This strategy helps students who become frustrated and "lost" when copying from far to near and vice versa.
- Use writing utensils with glitter/oil inside or placing a lava lamp or glitter tube near the student.
- Popular sites have recipes for making water bottles into calming visual aids for students. Place water, oil, glitter, sequins, and more into the bottle and glue the cap on. Let students keep them at their desks, shake them up, and watch the materials settle for a visual break.
- Cut cardboard with a "window" to fit only the words being read or the area the student needs to look at. This can help students who get overwhelmed visually.

Auditory (Hearing) Accommodations

- The benefits of listening to music during home or schoolwork can be calming. Music from classical composers, such as Mozart has been researched for its calming effect. There are many different rhythms and CDs available. One of my favorites is the CD *Sacred Earth Drums* by David and Steve Gordon. It's readily available on Amazon.com. The calming beats that are low frequency can be extremely relaxing, but I strongly urge students not to listen with headphones but instead play in open air. In our clinic we even march, dance, use long streams of colorful fabric and dance and move to the music. This can be done in larger classrooms or the gym for a movement break.

- Therapists who are trained in the "Listening with Your Whole Body" program are able to incorporate therapeutic listening CDs via headphones to students. The CDs are designed to target specific body systems, but are to be started and monitored closely by a trained therapist. To find a therapist near you, visit www.VitalLinks.net and click on "Find a Practitioner."

- Noise cancelling headphones may be issued for changing of classes/ hallway noise or for fire drills. The aide or teacher can simply give a visual cue or instruction to place the headphones over the ears prior to a "noisy" event. Some children benefit from the use of noise cancelling headphones during testing.

- The use of white noise machines may be calming to the entire classroom. They may block noises coming from outside in the hallway.

- I keep a fountain in my work area. The sound of running water can be quite calming. If permitted, purchase a small fountain for your classroom/study area. Sometimes, smooth rocks can be added to manipulate the sound of the water slightly.

Don't Forget the Nose! (Olfactory Accommodations)

Input we receive from our noses can alert us to danger, such as when we smell smoke or something burning. We often associate scents with pleasant memories. This is often the case when we smell a turkey or bread baking in the oven. However, smells can also retrieve bad memories. There is a direct link to our noses and the olfactory nerve. Our brains have an "olfactory bulb" which is part of the limbic system. This part is often called our "emotional brain" because it's tied to emotions and feelings. The interesting thing is that the olfactory bulb communicates with other parts of the brain which process memories and emotions. When we smell something we link it in our brains to that event, people and even the things we see around us at that time. This means that next time when we smell that same thing, memories and even emotions remind us of that or other past experiences—good and bad. Wow! This has always been quite amazing to me. It's critical to consider how different scents may affect our students.

- Consider smells in the classroom. I'm always mindful of any perfume, body lotion, or hair products I'm using with the students I work with. Some can detect any small changes in soaps and smells.
- Scents such as lavender and vanilla are calming and cinnamon and peppermint alert the senses. Use of scented oils are becoming popular. The oils can be used along with a diffuser to quickly spread their scent into the air. Allergies may be a concern, so check with parents first.
- Smencils (www.smencils.com) are scented pencils. The company is branching out to other writing tools which are scented. The best thing is that they are made of recycled newspaper! They range in scents and can be purchased at most teaching supply stores. I also use Mr. Marker's scented markers (purchased at most discount or office supply stores) for my students. It's a bonus to be able to smell what they are writing with!

Cafeteria Modifications

- Use ear plugs to minimize noise.
- Organize a lunch buddy system. The buddies help each other with trays, drinks, opening/closing containers, etc.
- Allow the student extra time if needed to eat her meals.
- Permit students to eat in a smaller and quieter area with a buddy or group of peers. This is a frequent accommodation I recommend.
- Pack lunches daily to alleviate oral sensory restrictions or dietary limitations. (See the next section for lunch ideas.)
- Allow students to push a cart and hand out lunches to peers.
- Assign seating or mark off student's table area to decrease unexpected bumping.
- Provide weighted or adapted utensils when necessary.
- Allow for weighted lap pads during lunch time to provide proprioceptive input.

What Is a "Sensory-Friendly" Lunch?

We can actually help our students to "organize" themselves more during snack and lunch time just by packing targeted items. Additionally, when we notice our students "mouthing," biting, chewing on non-food items, we can offer one of these specially targeted foods. It's important to consider that chewing is a wonderful way to gain proprioceptive input. The awesome thing is that we can use tastes, temperatures, textures, and flavors to give additional stimulation to the mouth! Here are some ideas I've gathered through the years:

- Crunchy veggies such as carrots, celery, peppers, and broccoli with dips or peanut butter.

- Chewy foods like bagels, popcorn, string cheese, chewy granola/fruit bars, pita bread, sourdough pretzels, and dehydrated fruit.
- Crunchy snacks include crackers, corn chips, potato chips, granola, and bagel chips.
- Bitter and spicy snacks "wake-up" the senses. These can include: hot tamales, small fire balls (the big ones pose a serious choking hazard), zesty chips, pepper, and cinnamon.
- Sour snacks increase saliva and can also be alerting. Examples include: Sour Patch Kids®, tear jerker candy, War Heads®, Starbursts®, lemonade, cranberries, and lemons.
- Sweet snacks are not our best options because sugars can cause many unwanted side effects. If students need sugary treats, here are some ideas: licorice, pudding, gumdrops, bubble gum, and lollipops.
- Altering the temperature can change our mouth and body reaction. Consider ice cream, ice chips, frozen fruits, popsicles, and snow cones.

Modifications for Gym Class and Extra Curricular Events

Classes that are not part of daily routines or are only for a semester may take additional time for any student to get used to. Our students with SPD may need some extra time and support. The following accommodations may be made:

- Use noise-cancelling headphones or ear plugs to decrease noises. The gym environment is usually one that reverberates sound off of the walls and causes echoes and sounds not normally heard. Allow the student a few days to process the setting prior to actually completing the activities in gym class.
- Keep commands short and place the student with SPD near the coach/teacher. Use visuals or a schedule board of the class's events for those

who are wearing ear plugs. Review the schedule prior to the onset of activity so the student understands exactly what's coming next.

- Use larger balls when working on toss/catch skills, larger bats for playing baseball, and slower moving beach balls when playing kicking games.

- Break down complicated motor tasks into smaller, more manageable steps.

- Consider that some students may not prefer the unexpected touch of other students, equipment, or balls that may fly in their direction. Allow for a "cool down" area of the gym where she may regroup or allow for a drink break to the water fountain or locker room.

- Remember that students with several types of SPD may have difficulty knowing where their bodies are in space. Some may even get physically ill with movement, especially when their heads are upside-down or against gravity. Offer support and encouragement. Encourage other students to "play nice" and not bully students who may not excel in sports. Everyone has different skills and talents!

- Be mindful of students who are about to have a meltdown due to unanticipated events. Formulate a plan with the special education team and write in the IEP to allow for the student's safe escape when she's in "fight or flight."

- Instead of using a whistle, try clapping your hands.

- If the student has difficulty with putting on/taking off clothing, allow him extra time for changing or give him the opportunity to have ten minutes to change prior to his classmates entering the locker room. This area is generally unsupervised and students may take advantage of locker room time for bullying. It may be extremely embarrassing for the student who has to determine which side of his clothing is front/back or to take extra time to button and tie. My son's school had swimming weekly. He had difficulty with dressing and undressing. Additionally, the students' hair got wet and needed to be dry prior to going back to class. I volunteered weekly so that I could offer my assistance and support to the teachers. By the time my son changed into his swimming trunks and donned goggles, class was half over! He barely had time to swim. When he was required to dry his hair, we had the additional hurdle of the sound of the hairdryer. We soon opened up his IEP and the team made wonderful accommodations. After that, he was quite successful!

- CDs such as *Sound-Eaze* and *School-Eaze* (www.pocketot. com) can help to prepare students for noises that are found in the community and at school. The CDs are not designed for headphones, but instead for open air use. The noises, such as gym class, swim meet, fire drill, and cafeteria are all set to basic rhythms so that the student can remain grounded. Encourage students to gradually turn up the volume as they are ready.
- Consider the temperature of the gym. If the student appears overheated, provide a rest break.

What Is a Sensory Room and How Does It Work?

Typical classrooms may be rich with colors, posters, and noises. The constant bombardment of sensory stimulation may be overwhelming for students with SPD. The teacher may notice an increase in negative behavior when a student feels overwhelmed yet cannot verbalize it. Additionally, with the increase of students with autism and sensory processing disorder, schools may greatly benefit from the creation of a designated space specifically designed with SPD in mind.

Remember, being proactive is critical to avoid meltdowns. When students with SPD begin to exhibit any signs of "disorganization" it is time to move to the sensory room. The sensory room is meant to be a supervised space by a therapist, teacher, or aide trained in the use and possible effects of the various pieces of equipment. Once a child has begun a full behavioral meltdown, it may be too late for intervention and safety may now be the priority.

As part of the IEP or accommodations list, visual supports such as the PECS (Picture Exchange Communication System) may be used. Pictures taken of actual objects in the classroom also work well and are an inexpensive alternative. Provide a picture card of the actual sensory room or provide a card with the word "break" on it. The card should be easily accessible to the student and should be handed to the aide or teacher when the student needs a break.

The other option is that the accommodations may list specific times where the student moves to the sensory room. For example, if the student generally appears lethargic at the beginning of the school day, a trip to the sensory room for some "wake-up" activities such as jumping on the trampoline or bouncing on the therapy ball may be beneficial. Alternatively, if the student has difficulty quieting or regulating her body after lunch, gym class, or recess; she may go to the sensory room for some deep pressure activities. Examples may include wrapping up in Lycra fabric, use of a weighted blanket, listening to calming music, or sitting in a smaller enclosed space such as a tent filled with blankets.

It is important that students learn that there is a purpose and specific rules for the sensory room. It is not an area for escaping work, but for regulating sensory systems. Occupational therapists will be able to explain which specific times of day a particular student needs to go to the sensory room. Collaborations with parents and teachers are critical to obtain data. A particular student may be better able to attend to a social studies or math class after a visit to the sensory room. It is important to make a schedule of the student's day and show him when he will go to the sensory room. Additionally, knowing the function of the equipment in the room will help students to make a choice of which activities work well for them. Supervision of a trained therapist is important to help guide students to the appropriate equipment.

Many schools simply do not have the additional space for a sensory room. There are many options such as an office which is rarely used or partitioned spaces in larger classrooms. With creativity and a good look at staff schedules, there may be an area that will work!

What Is Included in a Sensory Room?

Sensory rooms can have many different types of equipment depending on space and budget. Color of the room is a major consideration. Cool colors such as blue and green are generally calming while warm colors—red and orange are alerting. Since the sensory room is generally used for calming, a cooler color may be beneficial. Other considerations are lighting, flooring, swings or suspension equipment, and sound.

- The sensory room should provide input or activities for the many systems of the body. Remember that the senses include: sight, sound, smell, touch, taste, position in space, and movement.
- Smells such as lavender or vanilla may be used for calming. Cinnamon and peppermint are alerting. Some schools use diffusers to move scents around the room. Essential oils are becoming more and more popular and are affordable.
- Visual input may be provided by: room color, lighting via floor lamps vs. fluorescent lighting, bubble tubes, fiber-optic lights, mirrored balls, projectors, and interactive LED light boards
- Sound machines, music, and headphones can be used for the auditory system.
- For calming input to the body consider: weighted blankets and pads, rocking chairs, bean bags, floor mats, blankets, wedges, pop-up tents, air cushions, large balls, ball pits, vibratory massagers and pillows.

- Pop-up sensory tents including LED lighting and larger vibratory chairs and equipment are available from websites such as www.spacekraft.uk.co in the UK and www.schoolspecialty.com in the US.
- Fidget toys and bins made of sand, rice, or beans are excellent ideas for a sensory room.
- Oral-motor toys such as the Z-Vibe®, ARK's Grabber, ARK's Y Chew (pictured on the right), toothettes, whistles blowing cotton balls through straws, and blowing bubbles are ways to provide input to the mouth (photo courtesy of www.ARKTherapeutic.com).
- Provide snacks such as dehydrated fruit, crunchy veggies, crushed ice, gum, hard pretzels, jerky, and bagels.
- Use twisty straws, coffee stirrers, and smaller juice box straws to drink from. Offer use of straws for sipping up pudding, applesauce, or yogurt for "heavy work" by the mouth.
- Trampolines are great ways to achieve linear (up and down or back and forth) input. Purchase the one with a handle for children to feel more secure and to provide stability.
- Suspension equipment and scooters are available for larger spaces. It is important to remember that generally linear movement (such as rocking on a rocking chair or swinging back and forth on a swing) is calming. Spinning and rotary movement such as that achieved on a tire swing is generally alerting. Since

every student's sensory system is different, their response to sensory input will vary. See photo for ideas of items commonly found in a sensory room. Pictured are noise cancelling headphones, a pop-up tent, oral-motor toys, air cushion, and fidgets. They can be purchased together or as part of the unique "self-calming tool kit" from Fun and Function (photo courtesy of www.FunandFunction.com).

It is critical to have the supervision of a trained therapist when using suspension equipment. Vestibular input such as spinning and inverting the head upside-down is the most powerful of all types of input. In fact, this type of input can last from six to eight hours after it's applied!

Transitioning Activities for Students with SPD

Transitions are difficult for many students with and without special needs. There are many accommodations that can be used for the student with SPD as well as with the entire classroom.

 OUT OF THE POCKET ACTIVITY

- The routine of the classroom should be consistent. Provide a visual schedule of the daily events with words or pictures. If necessary, tape a copy of the schedule on the student's desk that is laminated and ask her to check off events after they occur.
- Use visual timers so that abstract concepts such as time may be visualized. Always provide a verbal warning as time ticks down.
- Provide praise and positive feedback to students who have successful transitions.
- Allow students to have a box with their tools for the day. Pens, pencils,

scissors, markers, etc. should be provided in the box to alleviate frequent movement from the desk.

- Use partitions inside the desk made of cardboard or smaller plastic bins. This will help to ensure organization.
- Use different physical transitions such as: crab walking to the next station, bunny hopping to gym class, walk backwards to art, or waddle like a penguin to the library. There are many fun ways to move our bodies without making noise in the hallways!
- Tape lines or paths for students who get confused or lost in the hallways while transitioning. Make signs for the student to follow. Allow him to create his own map of the school.
- Create an obstacle course for students as they move from place to place. Some ideas include crawling under the desk (pretend it's a bridge); taping off shapes or stepping stones (pretend students are in a lake and they don't want to "fall in"); or a hopscotch carpet or tape on floor.
- Use sayings such as, teacher says, "All Set?" and students reply, "You Bet!" to make sure students are listening prior to transitioning. Sometimes humming a certain song prior to transition time provides a great auditory cue of upcoming changes.
- Practice transitions to new areas or after semester breaks and quarterly changes in schedule. The unknown may cause anxiety for students who have schedule changes.
- Modify students' schedules to transition out of the classroom during back to back classes. For example, therapy time and library time one after the other alleviates moving back to the original classroom and then out again.
- Use a daily planner to provide a checklist so the student can write any changes for easy review. Ask teacher, student, and then parents to initial changes to ensure that the student has reviewed them.

- Give students a picture of which activity, class, or station is next. For example, hand a picture of art supplies for transition to art class. Ask the student to carry the picture with him and hand to the art teacher. Sometimes the physical item to carry is helpful when transitioning. This works well with older students who use passes to leave the classroom.
- Provide transition buddies. Peer support is a wonderful way to support students. The buddies can verbalize or make a fun gesture to each other when it's transition time.

It is important to ensure that students understand the rules of use for any sensory equipment listed in this book. Set your own rules and expectations for each student using equipment so that abuse of it does not take place. Many teachers and therapists provide the opportunity for all of the students in the classroom to try equipment such as the standing desk, air cushions, water bottles, etc. to remove the "novelty" or "mystery" of them. Also, it's important not to isolate students who need these wonderful accommodations. Providing a few of them for other classmates to use at the same time is a great way to do this.

Chapter 6 Resources

www.achievementproducts.com	Achievement Products
www.asensorylife.com	A Sensory Life
www.allthepossibilities.com	All The Possibilities
www.arktherapeutic.com	Ark Therapeutic
www.chewigem.com	Chewigem
www.vs.de/en/hokki	Hokki Stools
www.dyspraxia.org	Dyspraxia Association
www.exceptionalteaching.net	Exceptional Teaching
www.flaghouse.com	Flaghouse
www.funandfunction.con	Fun and Function
www.gregandsteve.com	Greg and Steve
www.Irlen.com	Irlen Institute
www.kidcompanions.com	Kid Companions
www.pocketot.com	Pocket Occupational Therapist
www.schoolmoves.com	S'Cool Moves
www.schooloutfitters.com	School Outfitters
www.senseez.com	Senseez
www.sensorysmarts.com	Raising a Sensory Smart Child
www.smencils.com	Smencil World
www.spdfoundation.net	Sensory Processing Disorder Foundation
www.spioworks.com	SPIO Compression Gear
www.therapyshoppe.com	The Therapy Shoppe
www.vitallinks.com	Vital Links

Chapter 7

Behavior and Transitions

What Is Behavior?

Often we think of behavior as a tantrum or action our child does to get attention. Behavior by definition in the Merriam Webster Dictionary [12] is, "a: the manner of conducting oneself b: anything that an organism does involving action and response to stimulation c: the response." Children respond to their environment. From birth, we are bombarded with lights, sounds, textures, and touches. It is our response to these things (stimuli) that helps us to survive in the world. For instance, when a baby cries for his bottle, his caregiver feeds him. He learns that his actions have consequences and then either repeats them or tries something else. It is critical to remember that behavior is the student's way of communicating with you. Koscinski (*The Pocket Occupational Therapist*, 2013) [13]

When a student performs a "behavior," he is exhibiting a reaction to and an expression about something around him. It is important to note that society determines some unspoken rules as to what is acceptable and unacceptable behavior. The creation of rules is critical to helping our students know exactly what to expect in the setting. Classroom rules and expectations should be clearly posted in an area easily viewed by all students. As teachers, therapists, and caregivers, we have the responsibility to help our students to succeed in their environment. Oftentimes, frustration can lead to behavior issues. It is important to note that having any disability does not exclude a student from following the rules of the school and classroom. We cannot make exceptions for aggressive behavior. It's for this reason that we can implement a behavior plan in the student's IEP. However, when a student does not understand the rules, we have a responsibility to adapt the way we teach rules to that student. The adaptations will be discussed further in the chapter, but can often include auditory and visual cues.

Does Every Child with Special Needs Have Behavior Issues?

You would be amazed at how often I receive this question. We all have behaviors! Some examples are scowling, laughing, stomping your feet in anger, crying, and yelling. As a parent of two children with autism spectrum disorders, I have the unique understanding of what is like to live and work professionally with children who have special needs. We have strict rules in our home and both of our sons are expected to obey them. Whether or not our children are verbal or non-verbal does not excuse them from following rules. Yes, it may be difficult to adhere to the social and unspoken rules, but the safety rules pertaining to the rights of the members of our home must be followed. The same is true in my clinics. Students are not permitted to hit, spit, or become aggressive toward our therapists. It is vastly different dealing with aggression from a 15-year-old than controlling a three-year-old with the same behavior. Many times, we suggest an aide or assistant who is uniquely trained in determining the specific student's signs of aggression and further how to keep the student and those around him safe. We have a safety plan in place with the numbers of those who are qualified to assist should the situation become dangerous. I recommend having a safety plan in writing and in place for all who work with students who exhibit aggression. The plan should be reviewed monthly and the team members should initial to confirm understanding.

Students with special needs and typical students sometimes cannot control behavior in the same way that you cannot control the knee-jerk reaction that happens during reflex testing. Some behavioral responses are simply reflexes. For example, when a person touches a hot stove, he reacts without thinking. Students with autism for example, may have difficulty communicating socially for wants, needs, and expressions of feelings and emotions. This may cause a decreased ability to communicate frustration and behaviors may result. If a child hears a fire alarm, he may go into a "flight or fight" response where he perceives the situation as dangerous. There are actually chemical reactions in the body, such as the release of the hormone adrenaline. As a result, he may flee the area looking for safety. He may also scream, push, or have an absolute melt-down. He simply cannot control this behavior as his basic instinct is for his own protection.

How Do I Analyze or Look at Behavior?

Children with special needs, those with sensory processing disorder, and typical children may exhibit behaviors that cannot be controlled. In fact, you probably have behaviors that result from frustrations in your daily life. What are some of them? Remember to consider your own responses to "difficult" situations or to things in your environment that cause you discomfort. Think about how you handle your responses. Some people chew gum or ice when they are frustrated, others yell or leave the scene to avoid the situation.

Consider the following about your own behavior:

- How does my behavior serve me?
- Am I getting something out of it?
- Am I trying to escape something boring or difficult?

- Did my behavior get attention? **Remember that sometimes negative behavior receives more attention than positive behavior does.
- Does it allow me to have some control over my life or surroundings?
- Am I in pain?
- What is good about my behavior?
- Am I trying to tell someone something (using words or not) with the behavior?

Students in the classroom may feel trapped as they simply do not know how or cannot express their frustrations. In order to assess a student's behavior, we need think further and spend some time being a behavior detective.

- Be objective.
- Consider the student's developmental level.
- Think about the student's environment.
- Could the student be sick? Remember the co-morbid conditions in Chapter 5?
- Is there an emotion that the student cannot verbalize, but is conveying through behavior?
- Are there speech and language or auditory processing delays?
- Is the activity when the behavior occurs a preferred or non- preferred task?
- What accommodations are in place to support the student's behavior?

What Is a Transition?

A transition is simply a change from one activity to another. A series of seamless transitions happens as you move throughout your daily routine, but you may feel disoriented on the first day of vacation or when in a new setting. Most of us can navigate the situation with some effort and transition smoothly. Unfortunately, children with special needs may have great difficulty with transitions. For example, students with autism have difficulty with abstract concepts such as time. If a student doesn't fully understand the situation, he may have increased anxiety which may cause a negative behavior. The magnitude of the anxiety increases when a child cannot verbally express the fear of the unknown or about an upcoming activity.

Be sure to ease students into transitions by providing them with a warning. This could be a verbal or visual warning. Timers that "show" time with a reddened area are available and are wonderful tools for providing a visual cue of time elapsing. Sand timers are also good; however, finding one that's plastic is critical as my students have thrown their timers in anger. Holding up two fingers and verbalizing, "two minute warning" is helpful. Finally, providing partners for transitions works well for children who are social and are motivated by their peers.

What Is an ABC Plan?

There are many students who have ABC plans in place in their IEPs. ABC is an acronym for Antecedent, Behavior, Consequence. The antecedent is the event that occurred prior to or just before the behavior. It can be how a task is presented, a transition, decreased attention from peers, a noise or unexpected touch while in line, a non-preferred task among many others. The behavior is the physical, emotional, or any noted change in the student such as a tantrum or full melt-down. C stands for consequence or what we do to deal with the behavior. Consequences may include: ignoring, punishment, removal from the situation, raising voice in disapproval.

It is extremely important when analyzing behavior to be objective and place your own opinions of the student aside. I am confident that there is always a reason why someone acts the way to do. It is our responsibility as caretakers, teachers, and therapists to determine the why.

Make a chart similar to the one on the following page.

Date/Time	Antecedent	Behavior	Consequence	Why? (Function)

- Describe the target behavior.
- With whom does the target behavior occur?
- What internal/external events occur (antecedents) before the behavior?
- What consequences were given?
- What was the possible reason(s) or functions of the behavior?

It is important to consider what has and has not worked with the student in the past. This will require investigation by many team members, including previous teachers and caregivers. Working as a team will form outcomes by helping with consistency in implementing the plan. What are the parents doing at home to discipline the child? What are their rules and how well does the student follow rules at home? Analyzing the student's strengths and weakness can assist in planning. Finally, consider that children often seek negative attention. This happens when we pay attention to a bad behavior. For example, a student in an otherwise quiet classroom speaks out with rude comments and other students laugh at her. The teacher stops his lesson and asks her to quiet down. She is getting attention from both the students and the teacher by acting badly. We do not intend to reinforce negative behavior but by the sole act of paying attention to it (and to the student/child); we have done so. Ignoring the behavior is helpful, but not always possible. It is important to plan a non-verbal punishment, such as simply placing an X on a strike board or a cotton ball (or other quiet reminder) on the student's desk. Three strikes, and you've lost a privilege. (But please do not take away a student's recess; it may be the only time she has a chance to have a sensory break.)

What Are Strategies We Can Use to Help with Behavior?

Knowing the specific learning styles of the students you are teaching is a first step toward working with their behavior. Providing the appropriate cues and instructions tailored to the student with special needs is the first critical intervention. For example, most children with autism spectrum disorders are visual learners. Verbally expressing the directions or rules will not suffice for these students. A visual cue will assist them in understanding exactly what is expected. There are many types of visual cues that can be created. Some teachers prefer to take actual pictures of the daily activities/items needed and then laminate them. The pictures can be placed in the order in which they will occur that day. As the student moves through the routine, he will either remove the picture or add a token to the schedule board next to the task he just completed. This idea can be adapted to each task. For example, if the task involves an experiment in science, the steps of the experiment can be shown visually either by written words or pictures. The schedule can be placed on the student's desk or used by the entire classroom to ensure the student is not easily identified.

When giving directions verbally it is critical to follow the following tips:

- Speak slowly.
- Give only one direction at a time.
- Make the direction short.
- Be specific.
- Tell what is expected, don't ask. "Begin writing" vs. "Are you ready to write?"

- Use a neutral tone.
- Exaggerate key words.

Most importantly, when the student does not follow a direction, ensure you follow through with the consequences that are predetermined. It is unreasonable to expect students to follow the rules if you have not been consistent in implementing the consequences. never try to teach a student during a crisis. Discuss the consequences ahead of time and review them often with students. Everyone throughout the student's day needs to be consistent in implementing the consequences and rules.

Token systems can be utilized to help reinforce behavior. A token system can be tailored to fit each student's specific needs. The student earns a token when he completes a task. There should be a goal to earn a predetermined amount of tokens to earn the reward. This is a great way to work on delayed gratification. We have adapted the token board for some students to rate their own performance on a scale. Red is not completed, yellow is incomplete, and green is completed. There are a pre-determined number of green boxes filled in at the end of the day to earn a reward. I have found that older students benefit from analyzing their own behavior and work. It helps them to become more responsible for their own behavior.

I also strongly recommend the "three strikes and you're out" rule. Make a board by laminating card stock or an index card. Place three Velcro tabs onto the board. Each time you give a warning, an x must be placed on the strike board. When three strikes are earned, the student has a specific consequence. It is critical that you review the consequence before the activity takes place so there's no debate if three strikes are given.

What Is a Panic Response, Meltdown, or Fight-or-Flight Reaction?

There are many times when our students have an abnormal or panic response to something that is considered non-threatening to most. This may be a sign of SPD (Sensory Processing Disorder) in one or more areas. The body's amygdala is the center where we process emotions such as fear. Our amygdala can actually get larger when we have anxiety and more frequent worry, anxiety, or panic attacks. Since our students may have experienced frequent failed attempts at functional and school tasks, they may worry or feel insecure when attempting something new or at which they have previously failed. The fear of failure may actually evoke the amygdala's response and cause a feeling of panic.

The sound of a fire alarm is designed to jolt us into a "fight or flight" mode. This is our body's response to protect us from the harm of fire or smoke. However, when we have the "fight or flight" response to the unexpected bump of another student, sound of a fluorescent light, or when climbing onto the playground equipment, the student may be exhibiting an abnormal response. Again, it is our jobs to ensure that we are detectives and help to determine why a student is having a meltdown.

What Is Self-Control?

The act of controlling your emotions and behaviors is self-control. There are many ways to help students develop this critical skill. It is important to remember not the chronological age of the student, but rather to consider the developmental age of the student. For example, if the student is 13 and in the eighth grade, but his emotional level is that of a 10-year-old, do not set your expectations for social skills to be that of his peers. Reading the IEP's evaluation report is critical to learning about the various tests that have been completed to determine chronological vs. developmental age.

Out of the Pocket Activity

- Assign partners to solve problems together. Give a problem and let them figure out a solution. Learning from directly interacting with peers in a real-life setting is one of the best ways to teach skills.
- Provide timers to students that show how long
- an activity will take. Having the visual aid is a helpful way to show students something as abstract as time.
- Encourage students to wait for the attention of teachers and other adults. This can be extremely difficult for students with special needs. Develop a cue such as a flag the student can put up onto a Styrofoam block on his desk when he needs assistance. He must wait until you come to his desk and remove the flag. The physical placement of an item can give the feeling of control to the student.
- Work on an activity as a class, such as a puzzle. Complete a little each day for a designated time. When the time's up, the students must move on to something else.
- Allow older students to problem solve (with your help) while watching others. This could be done at recess while observing other students. Encourage students to observe others who are waiting for their turn or who are exhibiting self-control. When the student has mastered this skill, encourage her to try it out with her peers. Let her build confidence by actually trying the skill and do not intervene or take over. Afterwards, discuss the student's performance with her and make suggestions or offer ways to improve for the next time. Letting the student choose from different possible solutions is a great way to help build confidence.

How Do I Channel Anger Appropriately?

One of the first things we teach in our clinic and during consultations with teachers is to determine what anger looks like for the specific student. As I mentioned earlier hitting, spitting, aggression, or screaming at others are all unacceptable behaviors. When students are angry—especially those who have limited verbal skills—communication may become difficult and behavior is the way these students "speak" to us. Channeling this anger is the challenge.

- Begin by establishing what behaviors are appropriate. Make a list of the behaviors and work with the student to demonstrate acceptable behaviors.

- Create a story that details what anger is and encourage the student to tell you examples of situations in which he becomes angry. If he is not able to verbally tell you, make an observation chart for a month and note those situations in which he gets angry. Let him know what you've observed. In the story, place pictures and as many visual representations as you can. It is helpful to have the student make the actual faces of his feelings so you can show him exactly what he looks like. Review the story frequently (with emphasis on the acceptable behaviors) and hand the story to the student when he becomes angry.

- Create an "I'm MAD or ANGRY" cue or sign that the student can give when either non-verbal or when extremely frustrated.

- Create visual cues such as a laminated STOP sign, picture of the sensory or calm down area, or make a specific motion (or stop in sign language) with your hands.

- Provide a safe place for the student to go if his behavior becomes out of control or harmful. The location must be discussed with all team members prior to the event that caused the behavior and listed in the IEP.

The student should know where to go and be familiar with the location. Make sure there are items there such as pillows, bean bags, calming lighting, or weighted blankets. Soft or relaxing music would be beneficial to assist the student in calming. Remember that no teaching should be done during a tantrum or melt-down.

How Do I Motivate Students (Especially Older Students) to Learn?

When children are entering school as kindergarteners, they may have an enthusiasm for learning that is exciting to teachers. As the years progress and the topics of study get more complicated and teachers expect more independence, the excitement of students may dwindle. As you may imagine, many students with special needs can become increasingly frustrated with school at this time. When my children were younger, I remember friends remarking, "Sure, it's easy when they're cute and little, but wait until they are bigger and things get difficult!" These comments resounded in my head as my children grew. There are many creative ways teachers and parents can motivate students throughout their educational journey.

It is our responsibility to provide praise and encouragement to our students. Every time they try a new skill, their success (combined with our response) can be critical for building confidence. We need to be good models of the behaviors we expect. When we are motivated to learn, it will be more exciting for our students. We should expect them to thrive and support them when they do not. Figuring out just how to do that is the trick.

- Encourage students to learn using a preferred topic. For example, it may be easier to work on a math word problem when we change the wording to a subject that is interesting to the child. Today, I adapted an algebra problem for my son (as I homeschooled him). Instead of using the reference to going to the dress store, as the original wording suggested, I substituted going to the football game. His interest peaked and he actually enjoyed finding the solution. In science, learning about density may be easier if we compare two train models or sports balls.

- Make your expectations clear and offer written or step by step objectives for the task. When the student knows exactly what's expected of her, the task seems less daunting.
- Ensure that each step has a clear starting and ending point.
- Assist your student in setting his own goals. Determine what motivates him to learn and what incentives he may need to achieve his goals. Self-monitoring is an important skill to learn early in life. Provide checklists as the assignment progresses.
- OTs have learned the unique skill of activity analysis. This simply means that we can break tasks down into specific steps and then adapt (make easier) the step in which the student is having difficulty. Activity analysis can be done when therapists and teachers investigate and determine at which point the student is not successful and begin one step earlier. Ensure success at that step and then move on to the next one. Provide praise and rewards as each step is accomplished.
- Take pictures of students as they are working in class on various subjects. Write an article for the school or community newspaper about the wonderful things your students are learning.

How Do I Help Older Students Learn What Motivates Them?

When students have difficulty with verbal skills, they may have difficulty expressing their feelings and emotions on paper. I have found that offering a limited number of choices is beneficial as it alleviates confusion and frustration. Here's an example of a checklist I recommend:

Statement	Always	Sometimes	Never
I enjoy school.			
I enjoy learning new things.			
I enjoy working hard when something is difficult.			
I wake up excited to go to school.			
I enjoy it when I do better than others in my class.			
I am happy when I'm learning a new skill.			
I think school is something that will help my future goals.			

As you may have noticed, the examples provided are for students who have an understanding of their emotions. The wording in the chart can be adapted to fit a particular student's needs. What is important is to determine if the student enjoys school at all and further identify what creative ideas can help the student increase his enjoyment of learning.

Chapter 8

Attention Disorders and Organizing

What Is ADD?
What Is ADHD?

Most parents agree that children have far more energy than adults. While this may be true, a student that has been having more difficulty than his peers in areas listed below may have ADHD. The term ADD was used in the past. Today, the medical community has agreed that the replacement acronym is ADHD (Attention Deficit Hyperactive Disorder). There are three subtypes: Inattention; hyperactive-impulsive; and combined inattention and hyperactivity/impulsive. Some of the many symptoms are as follows:

- difficulty focusing;
- difficulty controlling attention;
- trouble with organization skills;
- fidgets and seems in constant motion;

- has difficulty attending to the task he's working on;
- is often distractible;
- messy work or school areas;
- discrepancy between academic performance and actual knowledge;
- misses details, instructions, or steps of an activity;
- is not patient or has trouble with turn taking in both conversation and activities;
- avoids schoolwork or homework;
- difficulty transitioning from task to task;
- cannot complete tasks which he's started or begins many tasks yet finishes very few;
- adults have difficulty with finances, household management, organization at work, time management, social skills, or frequent errors both at work and home;
- can focus on preferred tasks which provide immediate reinforcement for prolonged periods, but have difficulty with those tasks less preferred;
- loses things often;
- moves as if driven by a motor.

One of my favorite websites is www.additudemag.com. It has checklists, research, information from childhood through adulthood, articles, a free magazine that's delivered to your e-mail, and helpful techniques for living with ADD/ADHD.

ADHD is not a learning disability. It's also not a myth, not imagined, and is not a "fake" condition. ADHD can be diagnosed by pediatricians, neurologists, psychiatrists, psychologists, among others.

It is one of the most common childhood disorders and can last well into adulthood. In fact, to have a diagnosis of ADHD as an adult, the symptoms must have begun in childhood. According to the National Institute of Mental Health: "ADHD affects about 4.1% American adults age 18 years and older in a given year.

The disorder affects 9.0% of American children age 13 to 18 years. Boys are four times at risk than girls." Please visit www.nimh.nih.gov/health/topics/attention-deficit-hyperactivity- disorder-adhd/index.shtml for more information.[14]

It's no coincidence that students who are entering school for the first time may be referred to an expert for diagnosis. Often times, parents do not notice that their child is any different than his peers. They may say, "Oh, that's just how Johnny is." However, when the teacher observes Johnny in class, she notes that he has difficulty with many areas indicative of ADHD. In other instances, parents notice that there's something vastly different than other children at a young age. Their child may have difficulty taking turns with siblings or peers, may demonstrate hyperactivity, have difficulty with emotions, or even seem to daydream. It's always best to ask your child's physician about any areas of concern.

In many cases ADHD is missed altogether. It may be subtle. When seeking a diagnosis, there will be many questions about development, social, behaviors, emotions, etc. The child will be closely observed by the physician while playing or doing a specified task. There are many questionnaires that are used for teachers, parents, and even students to assist in making the appropriate diagnosis. Also, a look at family history is completed since ADHD may be linked to heredity. There is no one cause of ADHD, but suspicions include: genetics, diet, parental smoking, use of dyes and additives in food, among others. There are many studies being done to further research into the growing field of ADHD.

It is truly sad that the child with ADHD may have been made fun of by peers or has been labeled as "lazy," "ditsy," "forgetful" and many other derogatory terms. This can lead to anxiety and depression. We must be careful not to give labels to our students with ADHD since they are well aware of their weaknesses. It's for this reason that we need to provide positive reinforcement and praise when a task or when a step of a task is completed. We should make jobs meaningful and attempt to relate homework and assignments to a preferred activity to increase motivation. Finally, it's critical that we find the areas in which students with ADHD are strong and help to foster them. This helps to build confidence.

What Are Executive Functioning Skills?

Executive functioning skills involve the brain's ability to manage many demands at once. When we think about the one brain that's responsible for our entire body's functions (those we are aware of and those we are not), it's easy to realize that when something goes wrong, many areas can be affected. The brain's ability to manage breathing, heart rate, digestion are those necessary for survival. We also have demands including paying attention to the task we're working on and screening out distractions in the environment and using our hands for tasks that are done daily, such as typing and writing. The highest level is when we are learning a new concept or skill, interpreting new information, socializing/conversing with others or working on difficult math problems. The wonderful thing about our brains is that we can complete all of these demands at the same time! We have learned how to use the resources we have (past and present) to successfully pull it all together!

Let's look at a task: When a student is assigned a paper, he must understand the assignment (making note of the due date and details of how to complete it), plan the paper out, manage frustrations he may have during each step of the process, break down the steps of completing the paper, manage the time necessary to complete it, and then do the work (research, writing/typing, gather thoughts, make outline, etc.). There is much more to writing a paper then we might initially realize! Now imagine you're in school and taking a full schedule of classes, each with their own assignments and tasks to be completed. It can be overwhelming very quickly!

Here are some signs that our executive function may be decreased: sloppy classwork, late work, forgotten homework, misplaced papers. This can be extremely frustrating to the student, parent, and teacher.

Just because a student has ADHD does not mean he is not smart! In fact he may be extremely intelligent. He may know the information, but not be able to complete the many steps needed to do the work. I was taught that our brain is similar to an executive assistant (formerly called a secretary). Here are some steps in executive functioning:

- Looking at or analyzing a task.
- Planning how to address the task.
- Organizing the steps needed to carry out that task.
- Develops timelines for task completion.
- Adjusts or shifts the steps, when needed to complete that task (may be ill on the day the task was to begin or when a certain step was due).
- Actually begins the task.
- Pays attention while working on the task.
- Remembering and considering the original assignment requirements and keeping them in mind throughout the entire task.
- Controls emotions and behaviors while completing the task.
- Changes/adapts to new demands or unexpected situations surrounding the task (desk breaks or the library book he wanted to cite is already checked out).
- Completes the task.

Whew, I'm tired just thinking about all of that! Can you imagine how your student feels when things don't go as planned and he is having difficulty in one or more areas?

How Can I Change the Way I Give Directions? What Is a Rubric?

It's important to adapt our own teaching methods for children with ADHD. It can be very difficult to understand too many words at once. When trying to attend to someone speaking, even if the student is listening at his best, multiple steps may be hard to process. Using different forms of teaching: kinesthetic (adding movement); visual (adding written instructions or visual cues); or auditory (use of sounds) can be beneficial to the student. Remember to assess how the individual student learns best.

- Break down instructions with many steps into individual ones. Ensure students understand each step.
- Allow students to repeat each instruction after they have heard them.
- Clap out instructions or add a rhythm or rhyme to them.
- Allow students to complete one instruction at a time and then come back for the next one.
- Use a written list of complex instructions. Use bullet points or different colors for each step and allow students to cross off each one as it's completed.
- Use pictures for each step if needed.
- Allow for a peer model to demonstrate steps for students.
- Allow students to highlight key words on worksheets and assignments.
- Provide outlines for students' lessons. This will allow them to attend to your voice and see the words written. Ask them to fill in blanks or key words.
- Allow extra time for following instructions.
- Provide steps written down on index cards at each center or task area. Give a picture of how each completed step looks as a model.
- Seat student near you to ensure he's attending to your instruction.
- Provide a rubric. Rubrics are becoming popular and being used in more and more classrooms. A rubric is usually a handout provided to students to let them know what's expected of them for an assignment. For example, a student receives a written assignment on George Washington.

The rubric outlines that the student must write a two page paper. He must do research on the life and work of Washington. The student must use the following: correct spelling, three references, correct punctuation, must be typed, discuss the childhood, battles fought, and presidency. Through the rubric, the student knows exactly what is expected of him. Additionally, rubrics provide structure that students with difficulty organizing may need. This is a helpful tool for any student!

What Are Some Class and Homework Accommodations?

- Use daily planners. When students are younger, they can use sheets showing the week. The weekly calendar should have the daily expectations clearly listed and a place for a checkmark, sticker, or reward when the tasks are accomplished.
- Write homework on the board. Let student copy it into his daily planner.
- Require teachers to initial the assignment book/planner and then the parent to initial when the assignments are complete.
- Provide an extra set of books for home use. Students do not have to remember to bring their books home and can concentrate on other tasks.
- Allow for increased time to complete assignments.
- Provide assignments, re-word problems to make them more meaningful to students, and use the student's specific interests for writing topics and math problems.
- Reinforce successes and encourage the student when she fails. Let her know that she's trying and it's through failures that we learn what we did incorrectly and what we can fix for next time.
- Provide study guides.
- Provide practice tests so that students know what to expect.
- Maintain a class website with homework assignments, due dates, and test

days. Update frequently so that parents and students are able to double check and keep up with classroom activities.

- Exchange notes with a buddy or set up study groups.
- Provide a phone chain or e-mail system so that parents can stay connected and students can ask for help when needed.
- Give options for extra credit or offer bonuses.
- Allow for a five minute review period at the end of in-class assignments and testing to ensure neat and complete work.
- Allow students the opportunity to use technology vs. written assignments. For example, make a PowerPoint presentation vs. writing a paper. Use an iPad to write answers on vs. using paper/pencil.

How Can I Help My Student Get Ready for School?

Parents are willing to help their students in any way they can. However, often they do not know what to do. Teachers also seek out information that is useful in helping their students. Understanding that everyone has the student's best interests in mind, let's review some helpful things to do at home and prior to the beginning of the school year.

OUT OF THE POCKET ACTIVITY

- All of us are required to wrap books in book covers. I remember when they were wrapped in newspaper or paper bags! It is a great idea to purchase a certain colored book cover for each subject. For example, reading books are wrapped in green and the notebook and

folders used for reading are all green—so each subject is a certain color. The picture shows green books, green notebooks, and green folders.

- Purchase a planning book prior to the school year. Practice using it in the summer with activities the student is involved in. Ask the student to show you his planner so you can make sure that he is using it properly. You can begin to initial the planner to acknowledge that you've seen it. The initial system is wonderful because the student, teacher, and parents can all follow the student's progress and know exactly what he's working on.

- Purchase a backpack with pockets and sections. It's much easier to organize something into smaller areas rather than it floating around in a big compartment. I associate it with ladies who carry large purses. It's very difficult to dig around and find any one thing because it all mixes together. Practice packing and unpacking the backpack prior to the school year.

- Use organizers, folders, and bins at the homework area. Make a "to-do" area and a "completed" area so that work isn't mixed together. Designate a pencil box for all school supplies including glue sticks, scissors, writing utensils, rulers, etc. This will help to stop students from getting up frequently to find lost supplies. Ask the student to write his name on his pencil box (or use stickers) to identify your student's supplies. I remember two years ago that I requested my son bring his pencil box home. I was amazed at how short and chewed up the pencils were. Additionally, I was surprised that 80% of the items were not even his. We quickly implemented a system where on Friday he brought his pencil box home so that we could restock and organize it together.

- Pack backpacks and review schedules the night before school. Set out clothing and supplies for the next day to alleviate stress and disorganization in the morning.

- Request an extra set of books and keep them organized neatly in a shelf near the homework area. Make sure that the shelving and desk area are neat and uncluttered at all times.

- Set up the homework area in a non-busy area of the home and away from distractions or areas such as kitchens, living rooms, televisions, and other children.
- Allow use of noise cancelling headphones to block out noise.
- Review the homework for the day when the student gets home. This way, there are no late night surprises. Break difficult or longer assignments down into smaller portions.
- Pick two equally challenging (or easy) worksheets or assignments and allow your student to choose which he will complete first.
- Provide reinforcements such as stickers, praise, or reward charts for extra motivation.
- Allow for movement after school and prior to homework time. This should last at least 45–60 minutes. If the student does not release pent-up energy, homework time may be very difficult.
- In my homeschool, we use rhythms and silly acronyms to learn new concepts. Adding a movement, song, or clapping to the beat of spelling words, math facts, and otherwise abstract concepts is helpful.
- Use visual checklists to scratch off homework items as they are completed.

What Are Some Accommodations to Decrease Distraction/Increase Attention to Task?

- It's always a good idea to limit distractions for students. Keep desk area free of clutter.
- Provide a schedule of daily activities, including any special events/ activities. It can be beneficial to provide students with a copied checklist

for their own desk so that they can check off activities as they occur.

- Use cardboard or desk dividers to make smaller areas out of the one large area commonly found within a desk. Sometimes, the vastness of a desk is overwhelming.

- Provide a desk corral around desk while testing or working on assignments.

- Use a non-verbal signal for the student when he's not attending. Walk by and tap lightly on desk.

- Provide hands-on learning or manipulatives. Many homeschooling students use the program *Math-U-See* because it has manipulatives that go along with lessons (www.mathusee.com). Teach abstract concepts with something the student can touch, such as tens cubes and blocks or magnetic numbers.

- Ensure students are listening by using a sound, such as a hand clap, tone, wind chimes, drum, rain stick, cymbal, and bell. I love the idea of using a response. An example is: Teacher says, "peanut butter," then students respond, "jelly." Use non-food ideas such as giving students a command to follow. Wait until all students are completing that command and are looking to you for your next instruction. Some teachers even have a silly secret word (like ocean or spaghetti) that otherwise wouldn't fit in the normal classroom routine.

- Allow students preferred seating close to the teacher. If distracted by other students, move desks away from each other. Don't seat students with decreased attention near windows, hallways, or play centers. Seating students near good role models can be beneficial.

- Use natural floor lamps vs. fluorescent lighting.

- Provide visual timers that count down time.

- Offer verbal countdown of time remaining for assignments or tests.

- Provide "brain breaks" for students after sustained attention. All students can benefit from this accommodation. See www.pocketot.com and go to "download resources" tab for inexpensive activity break pintables.

Are There Social Modifications?

Any student can have difficulty with social skills. When a student has a barrier to communication such as a speech delay or prior unsuccessful interactions with others, his self-esteem may be affected. Remember that our skills all build upon each other and when we have not experienced success or have had repeated failures with something, our self-esteem may be low. Often times, students with ADHD have had a difficult time socially or with other tasks. They may show signs of anxiety or sadness. We can identify this and help to increase their confidence.

- Social goals are common in IEPs and 504 plans. They can be accomplished in a variety of ways and settings. For example, a group of targeted students can have lunch at a table or in the guidance office. Peer buddies can be assigned, so that the student isn't isolated and doesn't feel singled-out. The entire class could have a buddy system. Buddies can be changed throughout the year to provide opportunities to model various students' conversational styles.

- Group assignments are a wonderful way to help students to feel involved socially. Provide time to work in groups in the classroom.

- Provide outlets for frustration that are age-appropriate. Examples could include a "cool-down" area; a trip to the guidance office to talk about frustrations/anxiety; give a job to student such as taking something to the library or office. The change of environment and brain break may help.

- Discuss behavior and social skills with student. Provide helpful tips for improving interaction with other students. Point out a situation which could have been handled better and then ask student for other appropriate ways to handle the situation. Remember, positive words work!

How Can I Help with Fidgeting and Movement in the Classroom?

ADHD, can have a hyperactivity component. Students with this need/craving for movement must have activities built-in to help them to release energy. Some of the information below is repeated from Chapter 4: Sensory Processing Disorder.

- Use fidget toys such as the Koosh ball, Tangle Jr., Fuzzy Tangle, or make your own out of fleece, burlap, balloons (often filled with sand or rice), and Lycra to place under the desk or in the student's pocket. There are many types of "fidget toys" available in catalogues for children with special needs or on Amazon.com.
- Place Velcro on the bottom of the student's desk so he may run fingers along its texture. I have added Velcro hook side to the desk bottom and the loop side to a wooden ball or spool. The student tries to move the items around underneath his desk from one side to the other without looking. Other fabrics such as burlap, velvet, felt, and cotton may be used.
- Pumice, sand paper, and other abrasive textures make wonderful fidgets.
- Place smooth stones in the pocket or in a fabric pouch.
- Wrap exercise band around legs of chair or two legs of the desk so that the student may gain input to his legs.
- Use "standing desks" with higher stools so that students who are unable to sit for long periods of time, can stand up. Try the "Standing Desk Conversion Kit" (www.flaghouse.com).
- Use foot fidgets, such as Foot-Shaped steppers (www.therapyshoppe.com) or Foot Fidget Footrest (www.funandfunction.com).
- Bean bags, "HowdaHUGS®" seats (www.howda.com), T- stools, rocking chairs, and ball chairs are all ideas for seating in a classroom.
- BOSU® balls are excellent for use in yoga, exercise, and for seating. They provide a great core muscle workout-awesome for proprioceptive input or heavy work.

For information on transitions, movement in the classroom, sensory breaks, please refer to Chapter 4. There are tons of suggestions and activities listed there for classes, lunch, gym, etc.

What Behavioral Modifications Are Available?

Remember that frustration may manifest itself in many ways. Behavior is communication! Students can have behaviors due to difficulty with attending to the teacher, completing their work, not understanding directions, losing assignments, being bored in class, etc. However, there must be consequences to breaking the rules and acting out. It's always better to look for frustrations when they occur and before they turn into behaviors. Communication between parents and teachers is critical for consistency.

 OUT OF THE POCKET ACTIVITY

- Post the daily schedule in the student's homework area and her classroom/desk. Knowing what's coming next and having some predictability is important. When the schedule changes (as it always does) provide as much warning as possible.
- Post list of rules along with the consequences of breaking them. Review them frequently and place them somewhere that is visible by all.
- Ignore negative behavior or inappropriate attempts to gain attention. For example, if a student repeatedly slides his paper off of the desk during your lecture; do not stop talking. Instead, deal with the student later.
- Provide a "cool down" area for students who become frustrated.
- Acknowledge correct answers only when a student has raised his hand or is called on. Do not allow speaking out.

- Make certain that consequences are consistent and are delivered to any student who breaks the rules. Often times, we tend to focus on our kids who have special needs and don't correct other students for doing the same things.
- Use a behavior contract where students agree to a list of appropriate behaviors and expectations. Ensure consequences are clearly listed. Ask student and parent to sign.
- Provide positive encouragement when a student is attending and behaving well. Frequent positive comments work much better than giving negative comments when a student is having difficulty! This is true for all students.
- Focus on the student's specific areas of strength and build upon them.
- Don't allow students to speak negatively about themselves. They may have heard negative comments and it's important that students replace the negative thoughts with positive ones.
- Providing students/parents with a report weekly (or as outlined in the student's plan) is a great way to work as a team.

How Do I Work on Goal Setting?

We all have goals for our lives. In fact, people from all over the world flock to the United States in pursuit of their dreams and goals. It is our job to ask our students what their goals are and assist them in determining ways to accomplish them. When a goal is not realistic, we should help students to make the appropriate changes.

The first step toward setting goals is to brainstorm. List all of the goals a student has, even if they seem lofty or silly. It's impossible to determine lifetime goals when children are younger, but learning how to set long and short-term goals is an invaluable skill we should teach our children.

1. What are the things you want to achieve today, by the end of the week, this month, year, etc.? What things are important to you and necessary for success in school? For example, a student who is in kindergarten may try to get through circle time without any verbal outbursts (with accommodations). An older student may have the goal of remembering his homework three times in a row. Goals should be meaningful to the person who is trying to achieve them. One of the biggest problems we face is that we try to set goals for our students and not with them.

    Additionally, we should make sure that we encourage students to attend IEP meetings when they are ready to help in their own goal setting. Every person's voice is important and children are no exception.

2. After brainstorming is finished, it's time to determine which goals are realistic. It's important to know that every goal should have a few basic components.

    - a time frame
    - specific (instead of "do my homework", write "complete all of my math problems")
    - a clear way to measure the goal and know when it's met
    - a plan or action the student must take toward the goal

3. Purchase a planner and write in it daily. Break down longer assignments into short, manageable steps. Often, when students see a due date for a paper to be turned in next week, they may procrastinate until the day before. It may be that the student truly forgets about the assignment and does not have the ability to break it down into steps. It's difficult to think about abstract concepts, such as time. This is very true for all students as they develop skills throughout school. Every one of us has probably knowingly or inadvertently waited until the last minute to work on a difficult task.

I suggest the following: If a paper is due in a week, begin by brainstorming on day one. Move to writing the main idea or position statement the next day. Progress to making an outline/structure of the key points in each paragraph. Create a rough draft, edit it, and then ask someone else to read it. Finally, complete the final paper. Write each of these steps in the daily planner on the day the student is expected to have the step completed.

Chapter 8 Resources

http://addiss.co.uk	National Attention Deficit Disorder Information and Support Service (UK)
www.additudemag.com	Living With Attention Deficit
www.adhdandyou.com	ADHD and You
www.adhdaware.org	ADHD Aware
adhd.kids.tripod.com	Outside The Box-Helping Misunderstood Kids
www.chadd.org	Children and Adults with Attention-Deficit/Hyperactivity Disorder
www.edgefoundation.org	Edge Foundation
www.mathusee.com	Math-U-See Manipulatives
www.ncld.org	National Center for Learning Disabilities
www.nimh.nih.gov	National Institute of Health
http://totallyadd.com	Totally ADD and Loving It

Chapter 9

Learning Disorders

What Is a Learning Disorder?

Learning disorders/disabilities are "invisible." A child with learning disorders does not appear any different than her peers. It is wonderful to report that a great deal of research has been done and is progressing toward a greater understanding of each type of learning disorder. According the National Center for Learning Disabilities website (NCLD.org) (15) at the time of the publication of this book "2.4 million school-aged children in the US are identified as having specific learning disabilities and are receiving educational support." There is no specific cause of the various types of learning disabilities and families must understand they their child has done nothing wrong. In fact, having a learning disability does not mean that students are "bad" or "difficult" in any way, but only that they learn differently. Specific techniques can be used to help throughout the student's life to help with the best functional outcomes. The student will have to employ different techniques to overcome their disabilities for the rest of their lives, so teaching them ways to help themselves as they get older is critical. Do not lose hope! Strategies are available and parents and teachers are getting wonderful information from books, websites, and publications geared toward a greater awareness and offering help for those dealing with learning disabilities.

I want to clarify that a learning disability is not the same thing as an intellectual disability. This means that children with dyslexia, for example, often have higher than average intelligence levels. The term mental retardation, now called intellectual disability, is associated with lower IQ scores. To qualify for an intellectual disability, a person must demonstrate an IQ lower than seventy, must be identified as such by the age of 18, and must demonstrate deficits in adaptive behaviors (two or more). Adaptive behaviors those things which allow a person to function independently at a certain age level. They also can be, in the case of someone with an intellectual disability, difficult or impossible to learn despite repeated attempts at training. For example: dressing, bathing, cooking, money management, sustaining employment, and so on. The needs of individuals and functional expectations change from birth to adulthood. The expectations of a student in first grade are vastly different than those of a college student. Cultural and societal beliefs also help to determine an individual's adaptive behavior.

Another difference is that learning disabilities are not the same as autism, a specific movement, vision, or physical disability, or sensory processing disorders. However, they can co-exist (and often do). It is important not to "treat" a diagnosis, but to consider the needs of the individual student.

How Do I Know if My Child Has a Learning Disorder?

There is no specific time for learning disorders to become obvious. In fact, sometimes adults realize that they have a specific deficit area in which they were never diagnosed! It is common in my clinic to have a parent realize that he too has ADHD after his child is diagnosed. It can be fun for the family to work together to help each other. As with any concern with your child/student, early intervention is key to helping as soon as possible to avoid frustration and provide early successes. It is my belief that the caregiver is the child's best advocate and should continue to push for testing to prove or disprove the presence of any specific issue their child may have. However, do not beat yourself up if you find out later that a learning disability is present. There are many strategies, therapies, programs, etc. available at any age.

What Are Some Signs My Child Has a Learning Disorder?

Throughout the following pages some specific learning disorders are listed along with common signs and symptoms. While specific deficits in reading, math, and other areas may be noted, do not ignore difficulties in the areas of social development. These include relationships with peers; psychological development—depression, anxiety, worry; or behavioral issues—tantrums and refusals to participate in activities. Learning disabilities may cause feelings of failure and the student may not realize what the root cause is. When failure happens (especially repeated failures), we are less likely to repeat the behavior and our confidence may be shaken. Many times adults themselves cannot realize or explain the "why" behind their own behavior.

It is critical to know that your child needs your support as the teacher, parent, caregiver, or therapist. Encourage students that they are not "dumb" or "stupid" as others may have called them, but that everyone learns a bit differently and they are no exception. Boosting self-confidence and providing successful opportunities are important to fostering the realization that students can and will go on to meet their goals in life. Yes, it may be a bit more difficult, but with the right tools, it can happen!

What Can I Do if I Think My Student Has a Learning Disorder?

 Out of the Pocket activity

Since learning disorders affect learning, they are most often realized while in school. As an advocate for both schools and families, I can assure you that a team approach is the best way to help students. I discuss the student's right for a free evaluation through the IDEA (Individuals with Disabilities Act) under which learning disabilities do qualify. (Chapter 1) You may also ask your school or pediatrician for a referral to a clinician qualified to diagnose learning disabilities.

I would advise you to collect some information about your child to discuss with the evaluator. It is always best to collect objective (not opinion) data. Facts speak for themselves, so make a list of things your student is:

1. great at doing/learning;
2. struggles with in school, homeschool, or when doing homework;
3. strategies you (or others) have tried that have worked;
4. strategies you have attempted that did not work (include negative behaviors your student had);
5. questions you have for the team.

When advocating for my own children, excitement often causes me to forget to mention a concern. Maybe you've experienced this in your car on the way home, "How could I have forgotten to ask that?" It's for this reason that I now write everything down. Use a highlighter or cross off each question or concern you discussed during the meeting. Just as with grocery shopping, you don't want to forget anything!

What Do I Expect the Evaluator to Do?

The evaluation will usually take a few hours and will look at family history, developmental areas, general intelligence, language or processing delays, phonological processing, math, reading fluency, visual-perceptual skills, writing, and other areas as determined necessary by the diagnostic team. In the school setting, often the assessor may examine the student in the classroom setting. The evaluation should be tailored toward your child's needs and address areas of concern. Remember, no child is the same and no evaluation is exactly the same. Make sure your child gets good rest the night before testing. Do not pressure her to do well, but encourage her to give testing her best effort. If she does not understand any portion of the test, encourage her to let the evaluator know.

What Do I Expect after the Testing Is Completed?

The report will not come the day of testing. There are many different assessments which use specific scoring systems that must be calculated. When the report is completed, it will generally begin with the history of your student's development, information about current concerns, names of each test used, results of each specific test, an interpretation of the meaning of results, the student's strengths and weaknesses, and recommendations. A team meeting should take place after the report is completed to discuss and implement strategies (known as accommodations in school). Refer to Chapter 1 for details about IEP and 504 plans.

What Is Dyslexia?

Dyslexia can be broken down into its Greek meaning. "Dys" means difficulty and "lexia" means word. So, dyslexia means "difficulty with words." Dyslexia is a neurological disorder which causes difficulty processing and interpreting written information. It is often difficult for people with dyslexia to identify separate speech sounds in words or realize how the letters represent sounds. Students may have difficulties in spelling, writing, reading and understanding words. Often times, they become frustrated and struggle academically if not identified and treated early. Just because someone has a learning disability, such as dyslexia, does not make them less smart. In fact, students with dyslexia are often very intelligent but they simply need strategies and accommodations to learn and succeed.

What Are Signs and Symptoms of Dyslexia?

✓ May be genetic
✓ Difficulty learning to speak, name objects, and learn alphabet
✓ Decreased interest in or difficulty with reading
✓ Trouble writing numbers and letters in the correct order v" Difficulty understanding directions (especially multi-step) v" Spelling inconsistencies noted in student's assignments v" Trouble learning spelling words
✓ Difficulty speaking and reading smoothly
✓ Reverses letters such as b, d, a.
✓ Hard to listen and take notes at the same time
✓ Social difficulty with pragmatics (body language, interpreting idioms, difficulty understanding jokes)
✓ Complaining about peers making fun of them when reading aloud or speaking
✓ Decreased self-esteem and difficulties in schoolwork despite high intelligence level.

This checklist is not meant to make a specific diagnosis, only to provide additional information for you. It is not inclusive of every symptom.

What Can I Do to Help My Student with Dyslexia?

- Enlarge the print on paper.
- Increase time to complete tests and assignments.
- Set aside a quiet place where students will not be distracted when taking tests. Noise cancelling headphones or earplugs may also be worn.
- Ask the library for books on CD. A fabulous site for recordings of books is www.learningally.org. It also provides additional information about dyslexia (including a great chart by age and symptoms).
- Use word-predicting software.
- Create PowerPoint presentations or iMovies of information to add interest and excitement to difficult information.
- Permit the use of word processor or laptop with spell check.
- Create a "perfect model" when asking students to write. I often suggest this with learning all new skills. For example, if reversing "d" is a problem, write an example for the student to reference.
- Break down assignments into steps. Work on each step bit by bit.
- Create multi-sensory ways of learning new things. Add body movement, rhythms, and color.
- Ask family members or friends to read or rehearse information with students.
- Encourage students to take their time when learning new material or studying. Putting pressure on the student may cause greater anxiety.

What Is a Visual Perceptual or Visual-Motor Learning Disability or Visual Processing Disorder?

This area of disorders is much more complex than simply checking for 20/20 vision. Students with visual processing disorders can have a perfect visual screen!

Many people struggling with visual processing never realize what the true problem is. This is why I highly recommend having a functional visual evaluation when a student is complaining of any difficulty seeing, reading, writing, focusing, headaches, and more. Visual processing disorders actually involve not only the eyes (or their movement), but also the student's brain and its difficulty processing (making sense of) the information that the eyes are taking in. It's not just an eye problem, it's a processing problem.

There are many different areas which are considered when looking at functional vision:

- Eye-hand coordination is the ability to use the hands and eyes together for tasks in everyday life. When we use the information we receive from our eyes to coordinate movement in other parts of the body, we are efficiently processing. Students copy from the board or a book by using visual motor processing skills. We coordinate our hands and eyes to do virtually everything, including handwriting, sewing, cutting, tying shoes, eating, and anything using hands and eyes as a functional team.
- Copying involves recognizing the features of a design and then drawing it from the model. Students copy from the board, to their planners, from books, from any visual source in the classroom.
- Figure-ground measures the ability to see specified figures even when they are hidden in confusing and complex backgrounds. Working a word search is a good example of using figure-ground information to find a hidden word. Finding an item in the refrigerator when it's full of food or a tool in a crowded tool box are functional examples
- Spatial orientation and spatial relation measure the ability to see how things are positioned in space. The difference between an x and a + sign and the difference in p and q; 2 and 5; reversals of 7 r, h, n, 3 and upper case E are examples. Considering that math and reading rely so heavily

on the relationship of items in space, it's easy to understand how a deficit in spatial relations can significantly affect a student's ability to function in school.

- Visual discrimination includes form constancy or the ability to match two figures that vary on one or more discriminating features—size, position, shade, etc. Comparing and contrasting shapes based on their similarities and differences is a skill for visual discrimination. Included are also the differences between colors, shapes, and patterns. Deficits in this area could significantly affect writing, reading, and math.

- Visual closure looks at the student's ability to recognize a figure when it's been drawn incompletely. We know that a circle is a circle, even when it's incompletely drawn. Another example is the human face. If the mouth is covered, we know and understand that it's the mouth that's missing from the face. This is a critical skill. Our brain can virtually "finish" or close an incomplete object based on what we know and our past experiences!

- Visual sequencing is the ability to see the order of things. If a student sees "was" instead of "saw" the meaning of the word is totally different. The same is true with number 1,234 vs. 4,321.

- Convergence is when we move our eyes towards each other when viewing objects in close proximity. Put your finger out in front of you at arm's length and then slowly bring it toward your nose. Your eyes converge, or move together to follow the finger's movement in a smooth way.

- Accommodation is when we shift or keep focus of our eyes on objects. This skill is needed when driving and copying near and far.

- Tracking is our ability to move our eyes (without moving our head) to view objects. Your doctor assesses tracking when he asks you to follow his finger as he moves it horizontally, vertically, and diagonally. Optimally, your eyes should move in a smooth coordinated manner.

- Visual memory can be broken down into long-term and short-term. Long-term is remembering something seen long ago, such as your first grade classroom, the way your first home looked, or remembering the directions to a board game long after reading them. Short-term memory is when we remember something seen recently. This could include having difficulty reading the sentences in a book. The other words and print can be distracting. In math, the other problems, symbols, and words are difficult to block out as they seem to "compete" with the problem the student is actually trying to work on. So, the student cannot remember what problem or solution he was actually working on in the first place. As you can imagine, this can be extremely difficult and frustrating.

What Are Some Signs and Symptoms of Visual Processing Disorders?

✓ Reverses letters

✓ Complains of "glare," "brightness," or reflection from the paper

✓ Uses whole head to scan papers/worksheets vs. moving eyes only

✓ Squints or rubs eyes often complaining of seeing double

✓ Words or letters may appear to move or float around on the paper

✓ Complains of headaches

✓ Can respond orally but not when asked to write answers

✓ Poor posture when reading or writing

✓ Sensitivity to light

✓ Has difficulty locating items in areas which are "crowded" such as: pantry, toy closet/box, among similar items, items in his desk

✓ Loses place when reading or doing worksheets

✓ Difficulty knowing right from left

✓ Poor spatial recognition or appears clumsy, often bumping into things.

Many of my students have difficulty with tripping on steps, sidewalks which are uneven, and curbs.

✓ Has difficulty recognizing small print or differences between letters and numbers which resemble each other. May make "sloppy mistakes" in math. Students are not trying to be sloppy, but they have difficulty lining up numbers in math problems and with addition/subtraction signs, etc.

Visit http://www.harmonyvisioncare.com.au/symptom-survey.php for a great checklist that is scored immediately. This may allow you to get an idea of your student's areas of weakness if he cannot verbalize them.

This checklist is not meant to make a specific diagnosis, only to provide additional information for you. It is not inclusive of every symptom.

What Are Some Strategies to Help with Visual Processing?

- Do not grade a student's writing, but instead grade the content.
- Allow for verbal responses vs. written ones.
- Provide a word processor and calculator as accommodations.
- Use a ruler, highlighter, or pencil to mark areas as the student reads and to help to keep focus.
- Highlight margins or use stop and go paper which is available to office supply stores or Amazon.com.
- Cut a "window" out of cardboard so that the student can move it as he reads or works the math problem.
- Enlarge print. Consider "friendly fonts" such as Comic Sans and Kristen ITC.
- See the section "Visual Supports" in Chapter 6.
- Website resources: http://www.eyecanlearn.com, http://www.visionandlearning.org, http://www.visiontherapy4kids.com (This is a vision therapy website, but has awesome resources and explanations.)

What Is Dysgraphia?

The word dysgraphia can be broken down into its Greek meaning. "Dys" means difficulty and "graphia" means writing. Dysgraphia simply means "difficulty with writing." It's a learning disability in the area of writing. There is not a cause of dysgraphia and it is important that teachers, caregivers, and therapists are familiar with its signs and symptoms. The student may have difficulty with fine motor tasks along with visual spatial issues, or language processing skills. Often students with dysgraphia are so worried about the task of writing that they forget what it is they are actually writing about. If not caught early, students may have difficulty as the task of taking notes becomes more and more important in higher grades.

What Are Signs and Symptoms of Dysgraphia?

Here is a checklist:

- ✓ difficulty with grasp on the pencil (may grasp too tightly) or have a grasp too close to the tip of the pencil;
- ✓ has difficulty with fine motor tasks/hand muscles;
- ✓ frequent erasing or errors noted;
- ✓ letters tilt or slant in many different directions;
- ✓ reversals of numbers and letters;
- ✓ gets tired when writing;
- ✓ writes slowly compared to peers;
- ✓ difficulty copying from the board;
- ✓ spelling difficulties—difficult to understand why language is good but spelling is poor;
- ✓ cannot finish handwriting assignments due to fatigue/tired hand;
- ✓ has difficulty with shape, letter, and number identification and formation;
- ✓ mixed print and cursive and/or mixed upper and lower case letters;

✓ difficulty with margins and spacing;

✓ may watch own hand while writing;

✓ illegible writing or letters formed incorrectly;

✓ inconsistencies in writing and spelling that cannot be explained.

This checklist is not meant to make a specific diagnosis, only to provide additional information for you. It is not inclusive of every symptom. **

What Can I Do to Help Students with Dysgraphia?

OUT OF THE POCKET ACTIVITY

- Use paper with raised lines to allow students to actually feel the lines.
- Teach cursive earlier since some students find the act of picking up their pencils for print more difficult than the smooth writing of cursive.
- Use a strikethrough vs. erasing when mistakes are made.
- Use graph paper to identify the space in which letters should be placed.
- Offer wide or narrow-ruled paper to student. Let him make the choice.
- Ask for a buddy note system or scribe, where notes may be exchanged with other students so that the student with dysgraphia does not have to worry about taking notes.
- Allow students to choose their own writing utensil. Sometimes a thicker pencil or addition of a gripper works well.
- Use multi-sensory techniques for learning letters, shapes, and numbers. Write letters in shaving crème, dough, on sandpaper, in the air. Add a texture to paper by placing sand paper or needlepoint grid behind the paper. See Chapter 3, section "How Do I Help with Letter Reversals?" for additional strategies.

- Allow for increased time to complete written assignments and lessons.
- Do not grade for writing neatness, all capital letters, or letter formation. Only grade the content of the assignment.
- Use talk-to-text or programs which allow the student to speak as the words are automatically printed.
- Provide assistance with editing.
- Use a recorder vs. taking handwritten notes.
- Encourage the use of graphic organizers such as those found on the following website: www.EnchantedLearning.com
- Apps, such as Dragon Dictation can be used. A wonderful list of apps. is available here: www.ncld.org.

What about Keyboarding?

Keyboarding is a reasonable accommodation for many students. There are many word processers available and some classrooms are using laptop computers or iPads in addition to the SMART Boards®. AlphaSmart 3000 is an example of simple word processing hardware. It's easy to use and has eight files for storing information. If you search activities for the hardware on the internet, there are some really fun ideas!

When students learn keyboarding, as with all new skills, it's best if they are typing something they enjoy. It is critical to begin teaching the correct positioning at the onset of keyboard use. Bad habits form quickly and when using methods such as using one finger to "peck" at the letters, inefficiency can begin. This will hinder speed and accuracy later on. Short session times with data collection are important. It's always best if the student participates in the collection of the data and charts his own progress. Additionally, ensure the student uses the keyboard across settings and subjects. Generalization is the best way to show mastery of a skill.

As an OT, I must emphasize that the student's hand and wrist position should be frequently monitored. The major nerve running inside of the wrist is called the median nerve. If pinched or subjected to compression frequently by improper wrist position while typing, carpal tunnel syndrome may result. A student's posture should be correct, and his feet should be flat on the floor. It's always important to ensure the table height is correct too.

Here are some beginning typing ideas: for younger children, provide a strip of their name and ask them to find the matching letters on the keyboard; ask them to go around the classroom or home and find items beginning with a specific letter such as "c." Ask them to type in the words. For older children; ask them to write about their likes or favorite activity in a few sentences. I do not recommend pressuring younger students to type at a specific speed requirement. My preference is to begin in grades two or three. Ask your child's OT what is recommended based age, coordination, visual-perception, academic level, and cognitive processing speed. There are varying guidelines, depending on the school district or the specific student's levels of how many wpm (words per minute) that should be typed. In fact, you may see a goal for a specific number of wpm on your child's IEP. This is a good and measureable annual goal.

What Is Dyscalculia?

In Greek, "dys" means difficulty with and in Latin "calculia" means to count. Dyscalculia means difficulty with counting/mathematics. It's a learning disability in math. Students who have dyscalculia are not less intelligent than other students. In fact, they may be advanced in other skill areas and only exhibit problems in math. It is also important to remember that dyscalculia affects every individual differently and changes with age. Visual-spatial (knowing where items are in relation to each other) difficulties may contribute to errors in long math problems. The student may exhibit "sloppy" work or make errors when transposing numbers within the problem. Some students have difficulty with language-processing deficits; they may have difficulty knowing what the words of math represent. Unless we are using a visual for every math problem, it is extremely difficult to get a visual picture of complex problems. Resulting difficulties can occur in telling time, losing track when it's her turn, and struggling when learning to play/read music. Everyone with dyscalculia shows different signs. It's important to remember that so much of our society is based on calculations, visual-spatial concepts, and time.

Here's a checklist of common symptoms:

✓ Difficulty with knowing the layout or where things are in relation to each other. Including directions, geographical locations, and getting lost easily.

✓ Younger children may have difficulty learning to count and may have trouble with knowing that numbers represent "how many" of something there are.

✓ Difficulty with skip counting (2, 4, 6, 8 ...).

✓ Time, speed, distance, and abstract math concepts are difficult.

✓ Lack of visualization of concepts such as the number line.

✓ Measurement, weight, temperature can be too abstract for the student.

✓ Trouble with "mental math" or estimating the number of items in front of him.

✓ Money difficulties may be observed later in life such as problems balancing checkbooks and keeping track of the family budget.

✓ Difficulty learning to read music. There are many "abstract" concepts in music which are difficult to visualize.

✓ Formulas and operations of math may be inconsistent from day to day.

✓ Student has difficulty with playing games such as chess that require strategy or visual-spatial skills.

This checklist is not meant to make a specific diagnosis, only to provide additional information for you. It is not inclusive of every symptom.

What Can I Do to Help Students with Dyscalculia?

OUT OF THE POCKET ACTIVITY

- Listen to your student/child if he reports that numbers do not make sense to him. Early identification is important as mathematical concepts build upon each other in school.
- Use graph paper that will model rows and columns so that students can visualize where the numbers belong.
- Use of a calculator is recommended for students who cannot complete "directional" math such as long division, decimals/percents, and algebra.
- As always, a multi-sensory approach to teaching numbers is helpful. Talk about numbers, jump on numbers you've drawn with chalk on a trampoline or sidewalk. Hop onto large foam numbers which can be as large as one foot by one foot.
- Math-U-See (www.MathUSee.com) is one of many curriculums which use concrete learning tools, videos, cumulative instructions, and manipulatives to teach math concepts. Their programs are adaptable and are commonly used in homeschools, special and general education classrooms.
- Draw number lines in the driveway or school playground and ask children to walk right or left to demonstrate positive and negative numbers.
- Exaggerate spacing between terms in problems: 9 + 11 = 20
- Add colors to code different columns. For example, ones can be highlighted pink; tens highlighted in orange, and so on. Make visual representations of abstract concepts such as grouping.
- Write the alphabet on the top of the paper. Now, circle the letters d and p. When converting from a decimal to a percent, the student moves from d to letter p, which is to the RIGHT. When converting from a percent

to a decimal, move from letter p to d, which is to the LEFT. This is an awesomely cool visual technique that is concrete and easy to remember! I recommend it often.

- If you're into the science of dyscalculia, Numberphile by Brady Haran is a great resource. It has YouTube videos and some of the latest research. As always, be certain to screen all videos/content in the internet prior to using them with your students.
- Use math manipulatives such as ones, tens, hundreds cubes. They are commonly purchased at teacher stores or on Amazon.com. Parquetry blocks can be used to illustrate fractions.

What Is Central Auditory Processing Disorder?

Auditory processing disorder and language processing disorder are two more types of learning disorders. Auditory processing disorder is also called central auditory processing disorder (CAPD) because it involves how the brain processes sounds that are heard by the student. A certain type of auditory processing disorder is a language processing disorder. Remember that language involves what information you receive (receptive) and information you give (expressive). Both types of language can be affected by language processing disorder. The important note is that students with any of the three disorders mentioned in this section can have a normal hearing screen/test. My own son passed his hearing exam at a local hospital with flying colors, yet is affected by CAPD! I am thankful that I had him tested by a specialist called an audiologist.

What Are Some Signs and Symptoms of Auditory Processing Disorders?

There is no specific test to determine true auditory processing disorder. According to the American Speech and Hearing Association, "it is important to know that, however valuable the information from the multi-disciplinary team is in understanding the child's overall areas of strength and weakness, none of the test tools used by these professionals are diagnostic tools for APD, and the actual diagnosis of APD must be made by an audiologist."[16] My son and husband have CAPD. It's interesting that my husband often speaks too loudly and I have to cue him to lower his voice yet my son speaks quietly since he lacks confidence in his verbal skills. They both experienced speech delays as young children. I have worked with many students who are also diagnosed. There are many variations and it's difficult to list all of the signs/symptoms. Additionally, it's difficult to tease out the symptoms of CAPD from other co-existing deficits. Here are some of the most common symptoms:

- ✓ Difficulty learning to speak or finding the correct words to use.
- ✓ Sensitivity to sound/noises in the environment. v" Seems not to listen or understand instructions. v" Difficulty filtering out background noise.
- ✓ Confusing words that may sound similar. v" Have a hard time sounding out words. v" Difficulty remembering lists of words.
- ✓ Trouble understanding idioms, jokes, and homophones.
- ✓ Can have low self-esteem due to frustrations and feeling like he or she is the only one struggling.

What Can I Do to Help My Student with Central Auditory Processing Disorders?

 OUT OF THE POCKET ACTIVITY

- Eliminate background noises as much as possible. See Chapter 6 "Sensory Processing Disorder," section: "Auditory Accommodations."
- Consider ear plugs or noise cancelling headphones for testing and during homework.

- Make certain that student's work area is neat.
- Work with student on letters and words which sound similar.
- Consult with a speech-language pathologist to set goals for students. Speech services are a necessary addition to the IEP for students with any of the CAPDs.
- Allow for use of a student planner so that assignments can be written down. Make sure the planner has ample room for the student to write.
- Assistive technology can help. Recording lectures or using PowerPoints that the student can review prior to tests to increase understanding can be extremely beneficial.
- Use a regular schedule and post any changes ahead of time (if possible). We all benefit from predictability and although life is quite the opposite, try to keep the learning setting as predictable as possible. Consider that the student is learning concepts which are new and difficult.
- Reduce distractions or position student near the teacher.
- Use kinesthetic learning (learning by incorporating movement activities). Hands-on manipulatives are wonderful as are movement activities. When learning math facts, add jumping, hopping, skipping, clapping, writing the numbers in the air with a glow stick, etc.
- Implement visuals as often as possible.
- Allow time to process. Give directions clearly and slowly. Write down specific steps of a task vs. giving the assignment in general terms.
- Emphasize key words with different vocal pitches or sing-songy voices. In my homeschool classroom, I stop talking until my son makes eye contact. After I have his full attention, I sing or clap out the direction and he mimics me. He loves it!
- www.kidshealth.org has a wonderful section on learning disabilities.

What is Non-Verbal Learning Disorder?

Students with Non-Verbal Learning Disorder (NVLD) often have high language skills combined with decreased coordination, social skills deficits, or visual-spatial skills. These students are often frustrated because they can express themselves well, yet get lost easily, have difficulty making friends, have difficulty with daily tasks such as opening/closing containers, tying shoes, buttoning, snapping, or zipping. It's critical to watch for signs of depression and isolation (as with any learning disability). Visit www.nldontheweb.org or www.ldaamerica.org for excellent information on NLD. It's important to note that research on NLD is increasing. Some clinicians have difficulty distinguishing NLD from the former diagnosis of Asperger's syndrome (which now falls under the autism category).

What Are Some Signs of Non-Verbal Learning Disorder (NLD)?

✓ Difficulty with tasks using the muscles of the hand (fine motor skills). These can include handwriting, scissor skills, and manipulating small objects.

✓ Gets lost easily.

✓ Forgets to do homework.

✓ Has difficulty participating in gym class or at recess.

✓ Appears to always "get in the way."

✓ Regularly misunderstands teachers and others.

✓ Needs frequent repetition of directions—especially those with many steps.

✓ Difficulty with math word problems or abstract concepts.

✓ Learns a task in the environment it's taught, but has difficulty generalizing it to another situation or setting.

✓ Has trouble with social skill cues such as reading body language and interpreting facial expressions.

✓ Depression is extremely common as students approach the teenage years.

On another personal note, my older son has NLD and has superior verbal skills, intelligence, and academic ability. However, he struggles in reading social cues, does not understand sarcasm, and is extremely naïve. In fact, one of his teachers had difficulty understanding how a student in middle school that appeared quite typical had such difficulty understanding social situations. Many students for which I advocate have similar stories. They are quite misunderstood and become very frustrated. It's for this reason that we must be detectives and try to communicate with each other to determine what the reason behind a behavior is. Remember, students may not know exactly why they are behaving in a certain way so we must examine behavior as a form of communication.

How Do I Help My Student with Non-Verbal Learning Disorder?

 OUT OF THE POCKET ACTIVITY

- Use techniques listed in Chapter 4, Fine Motor Skills, to work on strengthening the hand muscles.
- Work on generalization of skills. Begin by teaching a skill with verbal and visual cues. Discuss the steps needed for completing a task and take pictures of each step. Talk about what can go right or wrong during each step. After the task is complete, discuss what the student liked and didn't enjoy about it. Talking through complex tasks is beneficial and helps to build critical thinking skills. Do this often and with any task that the student finds interesting. Now, complete that same task in different locations to ensure your student truly understands how to complete it in all settings (generalization).
- It's difficult for students with NVLD to see the "whole picture" so discuss not only the individual steps of an idea or job, but how it will actually look when completed. For example, if the student wants to have a chess

club after school, encourage him to think about the how, when, where, who, why, cost, etc. Thinking through is often difficult but is a critical process to follow as life continues after school. When securing and maintaining a job, older students will need to demonstrate competency in this area.

- Help students with concepts such as turn-taking during games and with peers. Stop frequently and ask the student to identify his peer's body language, feelings, facial expressions, etc. Ask the peer to do the same.
- Monitor relationships with peers (when possible) and add social goals to the IEP. They should include having regard for others' personal space, learning body language, learning how much verbalization is too much (turn-taking in conversation), knowing idioms and nuisances of pragmatic language. Students with NVLD often have very few friends. They may get along well with teachers, but have difficulty interacting with peers.
- Assist students to consider both long and short-term consequences of his actions. List them if necessary and talk about decisions before making them.

Problem solving and critical thinking can be built this way.

- Provide a safe place for the student to go when frustrated, to process information, and to calm down. Knowing exactly where she can feel safe and talk about her feelings can be extremely beneficial and helps to prevent further anxiety and depression. Ask her to journal about her feelings.
- Teach organizational skills and how to break tasks down into steps.
- Review Chapter 7 on behavior for helpful tips on dealing with a student's frustration.

Chapter 9 Resources

www.aota.org	American Occupational Therapy Association
www.asha.org	American Speech-Language-Hearing Association
www.bdadyslexia.org.uk	British Dyslexia Assn
www.brainbalancecenters.com	Brain Balance Centers
www.dyscalculiaforum.com	Dyscalculia Forum
www.dyscalculia.org	Dyscalculia Site
www.dyslexia.ca	Dyslexia Resources Canada
www.dyslexia.com	Internet Circle of Friends (Dyslexia the Gift) International
www.dyslexickids.net	Dyslexic Kids
www.dyslexiascotland.org.uk	Dyslexia Scotland
www.dyspraxiaUSA.org	Dyspraxia Foundation USA
www.familyresourcenetwork.org	Family Resource Network
www.harmonyvisioncare.com.au	Harmony Vision
www.interdys.org	International Dyslexia Assn
www.kidshealth.org	Kids Health
www.ldamerica.org	Learning Disabilities Assn of America
www.ldresources.com	LD Resources
www.learningally.org	Learning Ally
www.mathusee.com	Math-U-See
www.ncld.org	National Center for Learning Disabilities
www.nhs.uk	Dyspraxia UK
www.numberphile.com	Numberphile
www.parentcenterhub.org	Center for Parent Information & Resources
www.readingrockets.org	Reading Rockets
teachingld.org	Teaching LD
www.visionandlearning.org	Vision and Learning
www.visiontherapy4kids.com	Vision Therapy 4 Kids

References

1. National Center for Learning Disabilities http://www.ncld.org/ Accessed May 2014.

2. Siegel, L. *Nolo's IEP Guide: Learning Disabilities.* 5th Edition: Berkeley, CA: Nolo; 2011.

3. Ibid.

4. Shellenberger S., Williams M. *How Does Your Engine Run: The Alert Program for Self-Regulation.* Albuquerque, NM: Therapy Works; 1994.

5. American Psychiatric Association, *Diagnostic and Statistical Manual of Mental Disorders.* 5th Edition. Arlington, VA: American Psychiatric Publishing; 2013.

6. Centers for Disease Control and Prevention.http://www.cdc.gov/ Accessed May 2014.

7. Miller, L. J. *Sensational Kids: Hope and Help for Children With Sensory Processing Disorder.* New York: Perigee; 2006.

8. Miller LJ, Anzalone ME, Lane SJ, Cermak SA, Osten ET. (2007) Concept evolution in sensory integration: A proposed nosology for diagnosis. *American Journal of Occupational Therapy.* 61(2):135- 140.

9. Tsakiris M, Tajadura-Jimenez A, & Costantini M (2011). Just a heartbeat away from one's body: interoceptive sensitivity predicts malleability of body representations. *Proceedings of the Royal Society, B, Biological Sciences.* 278(1717):2470-6.

10. Fisher, Murray & Bundy, *Sensory Integration: Theory and Practice.* 1991, F.A. Davis Company, p. 141(10).

11. Miller, L.J., Collins, B. Sensory Solutions: Sensory –Based Motor Disorders: Postural Disorder *Autism Asperger's Digest* (2012, Jul/Aug.):46-47.

12. Merriam-Webster Dictionary. http://www.merriam- webster.com/dictionary/behavior. Accessed May 2014.

13. Koscinski, C. *The Pocket Occupational Therapist.* London, England: Jessica Kingsley Publishers; 2013.

14. National Institutes of Health http://www.nimh.nih.gov/health/topics/attention-deficit- hyperactivity-disorder-adhd/index.shtml. Accessed May 2014.

15. National Center for Learning Disabilities http://ncld.org/types- learning-disabilities/what-is-ld. Accessed May 2014.

References

16. Bellis, T. J. *Understanding Auditory Processing Disorders in Children.* www. asha.org Accessed May 2014

17. Case-Smith J. Bryan T. The effects of occupational therapy with sensory integration emphasis on preschool-age children with autism. *American Journal of Occupational Therapy.* 1999; 53(5):489- 497.

18. Individuals with Disabilities Education Act and Individuals with Disabilities Education Improvement Act, 1997, Public Law 105- 1

About the Author

Cara Koscinski has her master's degree in Occupational Therapy and has been an occupational therapist since 1997. She is a homeschooling mother to her own two children with autism, sensory processing disorder, learning disabilities, and medically complex needs. In 2005, she was one of the founders of Aspire Pediatric Therapy, LLC and Route2Greatness, LLC.

As the Pocket Occupational Therapist, Cara provides occupational therapy services, advocacy, and consultations to school districts, church organizations, homeschoolers, and trainings to therapists in many disciplines. Cara was a speaker at the West Virginia Speech and Hearing Association state conference. She has also provided many continuing education modules, which are sold across the United States by HomeCEUConnection.com. Cara's company also creates, produces, and distributes CDs for children with auditory sensitivity, and designs and distributes autism, sensory processing disorder, and eosinophilic disease awareness products. The CDs that Cara has created, *Sound-Eaze* and *School-Eaze*, are featured in several catalogues for children with special needs, including: Southpaw Enterprises, Amazon, Abilitations, The Therapy Shoppe, and Achievement Products.

Cara is passionate about providing quality treatment to children with special needs, which is evident by her additional training and drive to seek new and fun ways to help children achieve their goals. By forming a partnership with the caregiver, goals for therapy can be met faster and while everyone is having fun!

Articles Ms. Koscinski has authored have been published in *Autism Asperger's Digest*, *Autism Spectrum Quarterly*, *APFED (American Partnership for Eosinophilic Disorders)*, *Something Special* magazine, and *NewsLine*, among others. Cara is an occupational therapy advisor to *Autism Asperger's Digest*. She was recently named as one of Jennifer O'Toole's Asperkids Advisors of Awesomeness. Cara was the recipient of the Duquesne University's Innovative Practice Entrepreneur Award and has served as an adjunct clinical instructor for the Duquesne University Occupational Therapy program. She has extensive training in sensory processing disorder, pediatric feeding techniques, tele-practice, school-based therapy, core muscle considerations, autism, gastrointestinal disorders, behavior, upper extremity treatment, handwriting, Therapeutic Listening®, caregiver stressors and support, visual perception, and business/private practice topics.

Her first book, *The Pocket Occupational Therapist for Families of Children with Special Needs* (Jessica Kingsley Publishers, 2013) was named an "Exceptional Resource" in the Fall 2013 publication of the *Autism Spectrum Quarterly*; was listed as one of the "Top 30 Books to Read if Your Child was Diagnosed with

Autism" by *Autism Asperger's Digest*; and was given "5 Stars" by the *Special Needs Book Review* (Sentio-Life Solutions). In February 2014, Ms. Koscinski was named as one of "10 Women Who Are Making an Impact on the Special Needs Community" by the *SpecialMoms Parenting* magazine.

Cara is a member of the American Occupational Therapy Association, is a licensed therapist in three states, and is registered by the National Board for Certification in Occupational Therapy with special emphasis in the area of pediatric therapy.

Notes

Notes